The Ultimate Keto Air Fryer Cookbook

THE ULTIMATE

Keto

Air Fryer

COOKBOOK

100+ Low-Carb, High-Fat Recipes

WENDY POLISI

PHOTOGRAPHY BY ANNIE MARTIN

ROCKRIDGE
PRESS

For general information on our other products and services or to obtain technical support, please contact our Customer Care Department within the United States at (866) 744-2665, or outside the United States at (510) 253-0500.

Rockridge Press publishes its books in a variety of electronic and print formats. Some content that appears in print may not be available in electronic books, and vice versa.

TRADEMARKS: Rockridge Press and the Rockridge Press logo are trademarks or registered trademarks of Callisto Media Inc. and/or its affiliates, in the United States and other countries, and may not be used without written permission. All other trademarks are the property of their respective owners. Rockridge Press is not associated with any product or vendor mentioned in this book.

Interior & Cover Designer: Michael Patti
Art Producer: Hannah Dickerson
Editor: Bridget Fitzgerald
Production Editor: Rachel Taenzler
Photography © 2020 Annie Martin
Cover: Chicken Parmesan, page 60

ISBN: Print 978-1-64611-568-6
eBook 978-1-64611-569-3
R0

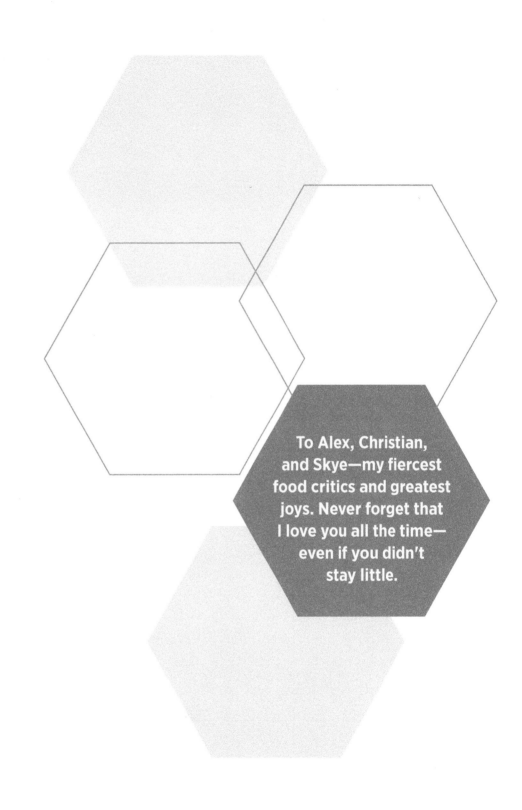

To Alex, Christian, and Skye—my fiercest food critics and greatest joys. Never forget that I love you all the time—even if you didn't stay little.

CONTENTS

INTRODUCTION

GROWING UP IN THE SOUTH, we ate a lot of fried food. I remember standing on a chair next to my mother, impatiently waiting as she fried chicken in a vat of shortening. I knew just how delicious that first crunchy bite was going to be. Back then, we didn't know much about nutrition. What we knew was that fried food tasted amazing.

Fast forward a few years, and I was entering adulthood as the low-fat movement was in full swing. Like most people, I believed the message that fat was terrible but refined carbohydrates—often in the form of some fat-free "healthy" product from a box—were just fine. With much regret, I said goodbye to fried food. In the years since, my views on health and nutrition have changed many times. I have tried every type of diet imaginable, searching for one that would leave me feeling my best. From vegan to paleo, I've done it all. None of them offered lasting solutions, and most left me hungry, cranky, and unhappy.

When I started hearing about the keto diet, I thought it was an exciting concept but that it was probably not any different than all the other plans I had tried. Imagine my surprise when I gave it a try and, within the first month, lost almost twenty pounds. *The same pounds that had refused to budge on a 1200-calorie vegan diet.* It wasn't just the weight loss that convinced me this diet deserved to be a lifestyle. It was the fact that my cravings were gone, my appetite was under control, and my energy levels had never been higher.

It was right around the time I was making the transition to a keto lifestyle that I got my first air fryer. I longed for crispy fried foods—and I wasn't disappointed in my new air fryer's ability to deliver. I did a little happy dance the first time I made keto fried chicken in the air fryer. I couldn't believe it when crispy chicken—chicken that tasted like it was loaded with carbs—emerged. Not only was it delicious, but it was also easy to make.

My air fryer made the keto lifestyle exciting, fun, and so enjoyable. In this book, you will find easy recipes with widely available ingredients. As a mom of three, I don't have time for fussy recipes, and I am guessing you don't either. While we will be keeping things simple, we won't be sacrificing flavor. There are few things I love more than the glow of satisfaction that comes from serving up a meal that the whole family loves. I am not willing to sacrifice that for any diet!

I hope you will fall as much in love with the air fryer as I have, and see that it is the ultimate tool to make the keto lifestyle easy—and delicious.

Sausage-Stuffed Peppers, page 129

1

Keto Air
Frying 101

What did you think the first time you heard about air fryers? If you are anything like me, you were intrigued but skeptical. Personally, while I found the promise of healthier fried food with little oil appealing, I seriously doubted that my investment in *yet another kitchen gadget* was going to be a game-changer.

Once I took the plunge, I was blown away. Not only does the air fryer deliver on its promise of deliciously crispy "fried" foods, but it also does so much more. It can cook perfectly roasted vegetables, a tasty breakfast frittata, and even my favorite desserts, all without heating up the kitchen.

As a bonus, the air fryer is ideally suited to a keto diet, because it allows you to dish up keto-friendly versions of all your favorite foods quickly and with minimal mess.

THE ADVANTAGES OF THE KETO AIR FRYER

There are many advantages to using your air fryer to prepare keto-friendly meals. Here are just a few.

1 IT'S EASY. You are going to love the ease of air fryer cooking. Except for the occasional flip, food can mostly be left alone once added to the air fryer. The temperature is well regulated, and many models will automatically shut off at the end of the cooking time. No more standing over a hot stove or babysitting oil to ensure it maintains the proper temperature.

2 IT'S FAST. Thanks to the appliance's convection fans, foods in the air fryer cook in less time than they do in the oven. You can expect to reduce the total cooking time by 20 to 25 percent.

3 CLEANUP IS A BREEZE. If you like easy cleanup, your air fryer will become your new best friend. You can say goodbye to oil spattered all over the kitchen and pots and pans strewn everywhere. Many air fryers have baskets and drawers that are dishwasher safe, so no hand-washing is necessary. (Make sure you check your manual before putting any parts of your air fryer in the dishwasher.)

4 IT'S PERFECT WHEN COOKING FOR TWO. While you can certainly cook for a family with an air fryer—and there are models that are specifically designed for this purpose—it is ideally suited to small-batch cooking. When you first embark on a keto lifestyle, you may have to cook one meal for your family, then a separate one for yourself. The air fryer makes this a breeze.

5 YOU'LL USE LESS OIL. Although fats aren't a bad thing on a keto diet, frying presents some challenges. Among them are the high costs of keto-friendly oils, and the challenge of keeping oils at safe temperatures. The air fryer minimizes your oil use without sacrificing the delicious results. (And there is no oil to worry about disposing of!)

6 YOU'LL GET THE BEST, CRISPIEST RESULTS FROM KETO-APPROVED "BREADED" FOODS. You can still enjoy crispy "breaded" food on keto (promise!), using alternative breading components such as almond flour and Parmesan cheese. These keto-friendly coatings don't adhere to proteins and vegetables quite as easily as traditional bread crumbs do (if you have ever tried cooking chicken breaded in an almond flour mixture in a pan, you know that more often than not at least some of your breading ends up stuck to the bottom of the pan). But, when you use your air fryer, you'll notice much less sticking and will actually get to enjoy the crispy coating.

7 IT'S ENERGY EFFICIENT. You are going to love not having to heat your stove or oven—especially in the summertime. Since air fryers heat up so fast and don't require preheating, you also save energy.

8 FINALLY, IT'S DELICIOUS. Thanks to the air circulation, food cooks evenly. You can expect consistently delicious food that will leave you wondering what you ever saw in carbs.

HOW IT WORKS

An air fryer is essentially a countertop convection oven. Most models are compact cylinders with perforated baskets that suspend the food in the chamber. There is a fast heating electric coil above the basket. Hot air is circulated around the food by a fan for faster and more even cooking. The intense hot air is perfect for not only creating the texture of fried foods, but also for roasting and grilling.

Although you don't need to use a lot of oil, most foods do best with a thin layer. With just a little oil, you can expect your results to come close to the crispiness of traditionally deep-fried foods.

CHOOSING AN AIR FRYER

The popularity of the air fryer has resulted in many new brands hitting the market. There are budget models that you can pick up for less than $50, as well as models that sell for more than $300. Which model works best for you depends on the size of your budget, the size of your family, and the amount of counter space you have.

Features: Pick and Choose

When shopping for an air fryer, it is important to start by identifying your must-have features. Once you know what you're looking for, it will be easier to find models that best meet your requirements. Here are the main features to take into consideration:

SIZE Air fryers range from small models that could fit in a tiny apartment kitchen, to XL models designed to feed a family. When choosing an air fryer, consider how many people you will be cooking for, the amount of counter space you have, and the clearance beneath your upper cabinets. In general, try to get the largest quality air fryer that fits within your budget and available space. The smaller your air fryer, the more often you will find yourself cooking in batches.

ACCESSORIES Some air fryers come with accessories, such as a pan, two-tier rack, and skewers; others do not. If you plan on using these extras—and I think you will—make sure you consider this in your overall budget.

PROGRAMMABLE OPTIONS Many air fryers come with presets that automatically determine the cooking time and temperature based on the type of food. Although some might find this function useful, the automatic cooking times and temperatures can vary by model, often making them unreliable. I much prefer to set my time and temperature manually, as you'll see in the recipes in this book.

DIALS The controls on your air fryer will be either digital or analog. I have had both, and I find that digital dials are much easier to use. This is a matter of personal preference.

TEMPERATURE RANGE Most air fryers today allow you to adjust the temperature, but there are some models that have only one setting. This limits the types of foods you can make with your air fryer and makes following recipes more challenging.

MAXIMUM TIMER Some air fryers will allow you to set a timer for no more than 30 minutes. Although for most recipes that is more than enough, there are some recipes that do require longer cooking times. Consider the types of dishes you plan on making and whether or not this is a factor for you.

AUTOMATIC STOP One of the things I love most about my air fryer is that it automatically stops at the end of the set cooking time. This means that if I get distracted with one of the kids, I don't have to worry about burnt food. This is a feature I wouldn't want to be without.

CONVECTION OVEN–STYLE In the last several years, convection oven–style models, such as the Breville Smart Oven Air, have come to market. These are larger than traditional air fryers, and they have additional functions such as baking, broiling, and dehydrating. They are great for large families because they eliminate the need to cook in batches. I have the Breville Smart Oven Air, and though I love it and use it every day for its other features, I much prefer my Philips XXL for air frying because I've found it delivers crispier food. The exception to this would be baked goods, like muffins, where the Breville really shines.

The Contenders

After you evaluate your needs, you can start to narrow down which model works best for your family based on the size, features, and included accessories. Because we are a family of five—including two teenage boys—I adore my Philips XXL, and all the recipes in this book were created using this air fryer model. The large size of the XXL helps eliminate the number of batches required to make a meal; however, it also takes up quite a bit of counter space. If you are working with a small area or want to store your air fryer in a cabinet between uses, a standard 3-quart model may be a better choice.

There are many air fryer makers out in the world in addition to Philips. They include GoWISE, Nuwave Brio, Power Airfryer, and T-Fal Actifry. Models can range from as small as 2.75 quarts to as large as 10 quarts. The temperature ranges and timer lengths vary from brand to brand and model to model, as do the accessories that come with the model. All brands have accessories that can be purchased separately, so you can have on hand what you know you will use, rather than a collection of less useful, nice-to-have add-ons that will mostly collect dust in your cabinet. Whether you're buying an air fryer for the first time or hoping to upgrade from your current model, it's always fun to do a little online comparison shopping.

Accessories

Air fryer accessories are a great way to get more out of your appliance. Here are some of my favorites.

AIR FRYER LINERS Although they are optional, I am a big fan of air fryer liners, which are essentially sheets of parchment paper with holes in them. They help prevent sticking and make cleanup a breeze. It is important to note that you should never put a liner in your air fryer unless it is weighed down with food. If the liner is not secured, the air fryer's fan can blow the parchment up to the heating element and create a safety hazard.

CAKE PAN AND DEEPER POT I have two 7-inch pans that I use daily. One is a shallow cake pan, and the other is deeper and perfect for recipes such as frittatas where spillover might be an issue. You can buy accessories that are meant for the air fryer, but it isn't necessary. If the pan is oven-safe and fits inside your air fryer, it will work great.

COOKING RACKS Cooking racks allow you to cook more foods at once by stacking them. A second layer of cooking space can help you avoid needing to cook in batches, and it's great for cooking a main course and side at the same time. There are also racks specifically designed for skewers, which make preparing kebabs a snap.

INSTANT-READ THERMOMETER One of the best kitchen gifts that you will ever give yourself is an instant-read thermometer. Because air fryers vary so much from brand to brand, the cooking times in this book are approximate. An instant-read thermometer ensures perfectly done meat every time.

OIL SPRAYER Although you use significantly less oil when air frying, most recipes will benefit from a spray of oil. Invest in a quality oil sprayer to make this an easy step.

OVEN MITTS Oven mitts are a must to protect your hands when removing food from the air fryer. I like ones that fit your hand like a glove and offer full protection. They are much easier to manage than bulkier mitts in the small space of the appliance.

PIZZA PAN Keto pizza is amazing, and there is no better way to cook it than in your air fryer.

RAMEKINS Chances are, you already have these in your kitchen. I reach for small ramekins when making desserts, reheating food, measuring out ingredients, and melting small amounts of butter.

SILICONE BAKING CUPS OR SMALL MUFFIN PAN You will find yourself reaching for these to make recipes like cupcakes and breakfast muffins. I use silicone baking cups regularly.

TONGS These are especially useful for removing foods from a hot air fryer.

GET COOKING

Now that you've got your air fryer and accessories, you are ready to get cooking. Here are the step-by-step instructions and hot tips you need to know to start using your new appliance.

Step By Step

New to the world of air fryer cooking? Here's what to do when you fire up your air fryer for the first time.

1 READ THE MANUAL. I must confess that I am often guilty of skipping this step. If you are new to air frying or have a new air fryer, it is important to take the time to read your manual. It will include information on how to operate the unit, plus safety tips and suggestions for how to clean the machine.

2 WASH YOUR AIR FRYER. Speaking of cleaning, remove the washable parts of your air fryer and wash them before using the appliance for the first time. Many units can be washed in the dishwasher. (Since you read your manual, you will know if this works for your fryer!)

3 SET UP. Once everything is clean, set up the unit on a flat surface with plenty of ventilation space. You can return the washed parts to the air fryer and turn it on for three or four minutes—the air fryer does a great job of drying itself! When you are operating your air fryer, make sure that it is pulled away from the wall so it can vent properly.

4 READ AND PREP. Read through your recipe and make sure you've got all the ingredients out, chopped, and measured before you start cooking. Don't forget to get out any accessories you might need, and keep your spray bottle of oil at hand.

5 CHOP EVENLY AND AVOID OVERCROWDING. As with most forms of cooking, chopping food evenly is important for even cooking. Food should be placed in the air fryer in a single layer. Avoid overcrowding the appliance, as this can cause foods to steam rather than fry.

6 NO NEED TO PREHEAT. Recipes in other books and online often call for preheating the air fryer, but because these appliances heat up at a rapid rate, I have found that preheating does not make a significant impact on the overall cooking time. Of course, every unit is different, so test yours and see if you need to preheat it.

7 SET A TIMER. Don't forget to set the built-in timer! Many units have an automatic shut-off, which is very convenient for avoiding overcooking.

8 SAFETY FIRST. If you are using accessories, I recommend placing them (and any food they're holding) in the basket and *then* turning the unit on. If you do need to place food in your fryer while it is on, make sure you protect your hands with oven mitts.

9 DON'T TIP THE DRAWER. When removing food from your air fryer, lift the air fryer basket from the drawer. Never turn the drawer over to get food out!

10 CLEAN THE WASHABLE PARTS OF YOUR UNIT AFTER USE. You can hand-wash them, but most models are made of dishwasher-safe components. I wash all the parts of my air fryer in the dishwasher every day.

Top Tips

Here are some tried-and-true tips for getting the most out of your air fryer.

AVOID OVER FILLING. When you over-fill your air fryer, you create cold spots where the air is blocked, causing food to cook unevenly and steam instead of getting crisp.

FLIP AND STIR. Most foods, with the exception of desserts and eggs, will do best when they are flipped halfway through the cooking time. For vegetables, either stir them or remove the basket and give it a good shake.

PAT PROTEINS DRY AND THEN SPRAY WITH OIL. For the crispiest meats, pat the surface dry before seasoning. Give the meat a good spray of oil, and then spray it again when you flip it at the halfway point. (The exception to this is marinated meats.)

PLACE PROTEINS ON TOP OF VEGETABLES. When you are trying to cook an entire meal in your air fryer, often it works well to put the protein on top of the vegetables. The vegetables benefit from being flavored by the juices of the meat, and this method can eliminate or reduce the need to cook in batches.

PRESS BREADING FIRMLY INTO THE FOOD. Air fryers have powerful fans that can blow your breading right off. To prevent this, make sure you press the breading mixture firmly onto the surface of your food. If you are still having issues, freezing the breaded food briefly before air frying can be very beneficial.

USE AN INSTANT-READ THERMOMETER. Because air fryers can vary so much in cooking time and temperature, I recommend using an instant-read thermometer for perfectly cooked meat every time.

CHECK FOOD. Because it heats up so quickly, the air fryer is very forgiving of frequent mid-cooking checks. I recommend checking on your food 3 to 4 minutes before the cooking time is done, especially while you're still learning how your air fryer behaves.

CLEAN YOUR AIR FRYER AFTER EVERY USE. Cleanup is never fun, but you will enjoy your air fryer so much more if you clean it after every use. Spills and oils at the bottom of your fryer can cause smoking, and may even alter flavors.

PROS AND CONS

The air fryer is great for fried foods, but it is also a versatile appliance that allows you to grill, bake, and roast. That being said, it isn't great at cooking everything.

THE BEST

VEGETABLES Most vegetables cook beautifully in the air fryer. Some of my favorites include broccoli, cauliflower, Brussels sprouts, and zucchini.

FISH, MEAT, AND POULTRY The air fryer really shines when it comes to cooking proteins. Prepare for a perfectly charred steak with a moist interior, and chicken so crispy you'd swear it's deep-fried.

BAKED DISHES Small baked dishes such as casseroles or even cinnamon rolls do beautifully in the air fryer. Not only is using your air fryer a great way to avoid heating up your kitchen, but it can also achieve better results than the oven does, thanks to the consistent temperatures and air circulation around the food. (I have a gas oven, and I use my air fryer whenever I can!)

(continued)

STEWS AND SOUPS Although you can melt butter or heat small amounts of liquids in the air fryer, trying to heat soups in the air fryer leads to quite a bit of splattering inside the unit.

SAUCES Portions of sauces can be made in the air fryer in some cases, but anything that contains or gives off a lot of liquid or requires a lot of stirring is better made on the stove.

WET BATTERS One of my husband's favorite chicken recipes entails coating the chicken with a wet batter and frying it in oil. This recipe was a disaster when I tried it in my air fryer. I suppose I should have seen it coming, but there was nothing to set the batter, so it slid right off the chicken and splattered all over my fryer. Even the heating element had to be cleaned before I could use the fryer again.

AIR FRIED AND LOW CARB

Air fryers are becoming increasingly popular because they allow you to whip up a delicious meal with minimal oil in a fraction of the time it would take you using other cooking methods. Best of all, you can fry, grill, roast, and even bake with little cleanup. Because eating keto means preparing all your meals, rather than relying on frozen and prepackaged foods, an air fryer can make your transition to the keto lifestyle much easier. This section is intended to give you a brief overview of the keto diet, not to be a complete guide. There are plenty of books out there that walk you through all the facets of the keto eating plan. Check out the resources section (page 180) for suggestions.

Keto Primer

The keto diet is a high-fat, low-carbohydrate, and moderate-protein diet that stimulates the body to burn fat as a primary source of energy.

To understand why this diet works, let's look at some basic science. Your body has two potential sources of fuel: glucose (or sugar) and fat. Glucose is a more accessible energy source, so the body will always burn it first when it is present. When you restrict carbohydrates and deprive the body of glucose, the liver will convert fat into molecules called ketone bodies. Ketones can fuel our bodies and brains just as well, if not better, than glucose can. When you reach the state of ketosis and become "fat adapted," your body can take your fat stores and turn them into energy. With fat adaptation comes a natural reduction in appetite, which can help with weight loss and blood sugar regulation (which helps you avoid long-term health issues).

Carb Substitutions

If the idea of giving up carbohydrates is overwhelming to you, don't worry! It isn't all that difficult, thanks to some easy low-carb swaps:

TRADITIONAL INGREDIENT	KETO SWAP
Corn oil, vegetable oil, canola oil, soybean oil, peanut oil, grapeseed oil	Avocado oil, coconut oil, olive oil
Margarine	Butter or ghee
Bread crumbs and other breading	Finely ground almond flour and finely grated Parmesan cheese
All-purpose flour	Finely ground almond flour, coconut flour
Milk	Heavy cream or unsweetened almond milk
Buns and wraps	Low-carb bread, cabbage leaves, lettuce leaves, portobello mushrooms
Crackers and chips	Cheese crisps, kale chips, nuts
Sugar	Erythritol, allulose, stevia, monk fruit
Rice	Cauliflower rice, broccoli rice, cabbage rice
Pasta	Zucchini noodles, cabbage noodles, spaghetti squash
Mashed potatoes	Mashed cauliflower
Lasagna noodles	Zucchini, eggplant (sliced lengthwise)
Taco shells	Homemade taco shells made with cheese

Macros

Macronutrients, or macros, are hugely important on a keto diet. Don't be scared off by the term—macros are just the essential nutrient contents of every food: carbohydrates, protein, and fat being the important ones. Tracking your macros may sound complicated, but it's simply making sure that you eat carbohydrates, protein, and fat in the proper proportions. That's it!

Although it is essential to track your macros once you first adapt to the keto lifestyle, you may not need to keep count forever. Each diet will look slightly different, depending on the individual's activity level, health concerns, genetics, and other factors. Here are some general guidelines for optimal macro levels for each meal:

70% TO 80% FAT

10% TO 20% PROTEIN

5% TO 15% CARBOHYDRATES

To get into the maximum fat-burning zone, you will want to keep your net carbs—which are the total carbs minus fiber and sugar alcohols—to less than 20 to 50 grams a day. Most people should start at the low end of this range and slowly increase to find their own personal "sweet spot."

For the purpose of this book, every recipe will aim to be below 10 net carbs per serving. Make sure you keep track of your net carbs each day so that you can mix and match recipes to reach your target.

Here are the answers to some of the most common questions you may have:

What do I do if my air fryer is smoking?
Turn off your machine and allow it to cool. Check for oil residue in the bottom and on the heating element. Clean all the parts thoroughly.

Why isn't my food getting crispy?

If you remembered to spray the food with oil, it may be overcrowded in the basket. Overcrowding creates areas of poor airflow, which in turn causes the food to steam instead of fry. It is also important to remember to flip the food or give the basket a shake halfway through cooking.

Do I have to use oil in my air fryer?

You don't HAVE to, but I highly recommend it. Healthy oils are encouraged on a keto diet, and a little oil goes a long way toward achieving optimal results. See page 17 for a list of the best oils to use when making keto meals.

Are cooking times consistent between air fryers?

Unfortunately, no. For this reason, it is important that you get to know your air fryer and adjust the cooking times accordingly.

What is the smoke point of oil, and why is it important?

When oil hits its smoke point, it begins to oxidize and create harmful free radicals. It is believed that free radicals play a role in the development of numerous health conditions, including cancer. Here are the smoke points of keto-friendly oils:

Almond oil	430°F
Avocado oil	520°F
Coconut oil, refined	450°F
Coconut oil, unrefined	350°F
Extra-virgin olive oil	320°F
Flaxseed oil	225°F
Macadamia nut oil	410°F
MCT oil	320°F
Olive oil	390°F
Sesame oil	350°F

THE KETO KITCHEN

Nothing can derail a keto diet quicker than a lack of preparation. The first step to success is planning your meals for the week and then making sure you have everything on hand that you will need. I don't know about you, but I don't have the time or patience to run to the store at 5:40 p.m. on a Tuesday and then come home and make a healthy meal. A well-stocked kitchen makes air fryer keto cooking fast, easy, and enjoyable.

Staples

There are a few staples essential for a keto-ready pantry. Here are my recommendations:

AVOCADO OIL Avocado oil is my go-to oil for air frying, thanks to its high smoke point. It is rich in heart-healthy monounsaturated fat and full of vitamins E and B_6. You can substitute another keto-friendly oil if you like; just be mindful of the smoke points.

BAKING POWDER Baking powder is baking soda that has cream of tartar and either cornstarch or potato starch added to it. I like Hain Pure Foods Featherweight Baking Powder because it is made with potato starch rather than cornstarch. (Cornstarch is often genetically modified and is a common allergen.) Either way, the carbohydrates added by the starch are minimal.

COCONUT AMINOS Most people agree that staying away from soy on a keto diet is a good idea. Soy is often heavily processed and genetically modified, which may stall weight loss. Coconut aminos, which is made from the sap of coconut trees, is a keto-friendly alternative to soy sauce. Most grocery stores carry it these days, and it is also readily available online.

EGGS All the recipes in this book were tested with large eggs. Look for free-range organic eggs when possible.

FINELY GROUND BLANCHED ALMOND FLOUR Almond flour is my go-to flour in my keto pantry. Make sure you don't confuse almond meal with blanched almond flour. Almond meal is much coarser and can contain almond husks. It will not work the same as almond flour in recipes. You should also try to use the finest almond flour you can find. I used Bob's Red Mill almond flour for the testing of these recipes; you can find it in most supermarkets and online.

GRASS-FED GELATIN We are hearing a lot these days about gelatin, and for good reason. Studies show that it is beneficial to joint health and can improve the appearance of skin, hair, and nails. It may even help with digestion. Not only is gelatin fabulous to add to coffee, but it is also helpful in improving the texture of meatballs and meatloaf.

MAPLE SYRUP SUBSTITUTE I always keep a keto-friendly maple syrup on hand. I like the flavor of both Lakanto and ChocZero, but ChocZero sugar-free maple syrup wins out for use in recipes because it is thicker and therefore better for texture.

STEVIA-SWEETENED CHOCOLATE Just because you are following a keto diet doesn't mean you have to give up chocolate. (That would just be wrong!) I am a big fan of stevia-sweetened chocolate. My go-to brand is Lily's Sweets, which offers chocolate chips and chocolate bars. You can find their products at some grocery stores, Whole Foods Market, and online.

SWEETENERS There are quite a few options for keto-friendly sweeteners, and all of them have their benefits. I am a big fan of erythritol-based sweeteners, which have zero net carbs, allowing for more flexibility than other sweeteners. Swerve is my brand of choice, and I also like monk fruit. You'll see an entry in the nutritional calculations for erythritol, which will help you compute your net carbs accurately. All the recipes in this book that use white sugar were tested with Swerve Confectioners sweetener. For brown sugar, both Swerve and Sukrin Gold have good options.

UNSWEETENED COCOA POWDER A good quality Dutch-process cocoa powder will go a long way to improve the flavor of your dishes. I like Guittard, which I buy online.

VANILLA EXTRACT Unless you are avoiding alcohol, steer clear of imitation vanilla extract. Pure vanilla extract has so much more flavor.

XANTHAN GUM I have been gluten-free for years, so xanthan gum is something I've been using for a long time. Unless you are gluten-free, it may not be something you are familiar with. In the absence of gluten, it helps act as a binder in baked goods. It is also helpful for thickening sauces. You can find it online or in the gluten-free baking section of most grocery stores.

Spices

These are the spices I use most often in my keto kitchen:

BASIL In the summer when I have an abundance, fresh basil is always best. The rest of the year, I keep dried basil on hand. Substitute 1 tablespoon of chopped fresh basil for every teaspoon of dried basil, or vice versa.

CHILI POWDER Chili powder is a blend of spices, and sometimes the manufacturers add additives to the blend. Make sure you read the label to avoid adding unwanted carbohydrates to your meal.

CINNAMON Ground cinnamon is like a hug in a jar! I like to use Ceylon cinnamon, which can be a bit more expensive but is loaded with antioxidants and has a richer flavor than regular cinnamon.

FRESHLY GROUND BLACK PEPPER I prefer freshly ground black pepper and use it for all the recipes in this book; it's easy to pick up a mini pepper grinder at the store if you don't already have one. Of course, sometimes we all get lazy and occasionally use ground pepper from the cabinet. (I'll never tell.)

GARLIC POWDER I like garlic powder for its convenience, but feel free to substitute minced fresh garlic.

ONION POWDER Onions are surprisingly high in carbohydrates. Good thing a little goes a long way. I use onion powder when I don't have onions on hand or I'm trying to convince my six-year-old to eat something and don't want her to immediately reject it at the sight of onions.

OREGANO As with basil, feel free to substitute fresh oregano for dried if you have it on hand.

SALT I use finely ground sea salt in all my recipes. Most often, I use pink Himalayan salt. To finish recipes, I keep flakey Maldon sea salt on hand all the time. Always salt to taste. If you use coarse kosher salt, you may need to add more to attain the right flavor.

SMOKED PAPRIKA I am wild for Spanish smoked paprika, which is called pimentón. It is a little bit spicy and adds a smoky kick to foods. Feel free to use regular paprika if you prefer.

TACO SEASONING Most commercial taco seasonings include fillers that can add carbohydrates to your meal. On page 167, I've given you a keto-friendly version you can make yourself.

THYME Thyme is one of my favorite herbs for seasoning vegetables and proteins. If you want to use fresh thyme, substitute 1 teaspoon of chopped fresh thyme leaves for every ⅓ teaspoon of dried thyme, or vice versa.

KETO OILS AND FATS

Healthy oils—including saturated fats, monounsaturated fat, and natural polyunsaturated fats—play an important role in a keto diet. That doesn't mean that all oils are good, though. Hydrogenated oils and trans fats should be avoided, as well as highly refined oils. My favorite oil for cooking is avocado oil, because of its high smoke point. I like to use extra-virgin olive oil for salad, and MCT oil (medium-chain triglyceride, commonly extracted from coconut oil) is great in your morning coffee!

OILS TO AVOID	KETO-FRIENDLY OILS
Canola	Almond
Corn	Avocado
Safflower	Coconut
Soybean	Extra-virgin olive
Sunflower	Flaxseed
	Macadamia nut
	MCT
	Olive
	Sesame

ABOUT THE RECIPES

You can expect the recipes in this book to be flavor-packed, approachable, and easy to prepare. Except for some keto-specific foods that I mentioned in the pantry section, all the ingredients you'll need can be found in any well-stocked pantry.

Although the recipes are straightforward, make sure you read them from start to finish before you begin cooking. I recommend prepping (chopping, cutting, and measuring) all your ingredients before you start, as well. This pre-cooking setup is called *mise en place*, and I find that cooking is so much more enjoyable when I take the time to do it.

Accessories

Some of the recipes in this book call for specific air fryer accessories. If your air fryer didn't come with them, they can easily be purchased at home goods stores or online. All these accessories should be the right size to fit inside your air fryer.

- Cake pan
- Deep pan (about 3 inches deep)
- Silicone muffin liners or a muffin pan
- Layer rack for kebabs

Nutrition Facts

The recipes that follow include nutritional information, and you can expect all recipes to be below 10 net carbohydrates or thereabouts. Remember that NET CARBS = TOTAL CARBS – FIBER – SUGAR ALCOHOLS.

When you are first starting a keto diet, I recommend that you aim for about 20 net carbohydrates a day. Once you reach a state of ketosis, you will learn how your body responds. Some people can maintain ketosis with 50 net carbs. You will figure out what works best for you—everyone is different, so everyone's keto journey is different.

Labels and Tips

To help give you a snapshot of each recipe, I've included the following labels:

- QUICK: 30 minutes or less, from start to finish.
- KID-FRIENDLY: I have three picky eaters—these are the recipes that passed the tests of all of them.
- VEGETARIAN: These recipes do not contain meat but may contain dairy or egg.
- FAVORITE: These are the recipes I find myself making again and again.
- 5-INGREDIENT: These recipes call for no more than five ingredients (in addition to salt, black pepper, and oil).

After you read through the following chapters, make sure you check out the tips I provide at the end of many of the recipes. The tips fall into these categories:

- SUBSTITUTION TIP: When ingredients can be subbed out for flavor or allergy reasons.

- COOKING TIP: Helpful info that may make the dish easier to prep, cook, or clean up.

- INGREDIENT TIP: More info about selecting or buying ingredients, working with them, or surprising/helpful nutrition facts.

- VARIATION TIP: Suggestions for adding or changing ingredients to mix things up a little or try something new with the recipe.

- AIR FRYER TIP: How best to use your air fryer, how to adapt the recipe, or how to combine two recipes at the same time.

Let's get air frying!

Southwestern
Breakfast Taco, page 32

2

Eggs & Brunch

Down Home Biscuits

PREP TIME: **15 MINUTES** | COOK TIME: **12 TO 15 MINUTES** | TEMPERATURE: **325°F**

Few foods are as comforting as piping hot biscuits! I make these for my family almost every weekend and serve them with keto-friendly Creamy Sausage Gravy (page 166). They are also fabulous for a Classic Egg Sandwich (page 30). This is one the whole crowd—even those not on a keto diet—will enjoy.   SERVES 12

KID-FRIENDLY

VEGETARIAN

FAVORITE

10 ounces (2¼ cups plus 2 tablespoons) finely ground blanched almond flour

1½ tablespoons baking powder

1 teaspoon garlic powder

1 teaspoon sea salt

½ teaspoon freshly ground black pepper

¼ teaspoon xanthan gum

3 tablespoons unsalted butter, melted, divided

1 large egg, beaten

¾ cup heavy (whipping) cream

¾ cup shredded Cheddar cheese (optional)

1. In a large bowl, whisk together the almond flour, baking powder, garlic powder, salt, pepper, and xanthan gum.

2. In a small bowl, whisk together 1 tablespoon of the melted butter, the egg, and the heavy cream.

3. Add the wet mixture to the dry mixture and stir, just until the dough comes together. Stir in the Cheddar cheese (if using).

4. Place the dough on a sheet of parchment paper and press it out evenly to a ½-inch thickness.

5. Using a 2½-inch round cookie cutter, cut the dough into biscuits. Ball up the dough scraps, press it out again, and continue cutting biscuits until all the dough is used.

6. Working in batches, place the biscuits in either silicone muffin cups or in a 7-inch cake pan that fits in the basket of your air fryer. Brush the tops and sides of the biscuits with the remaining 2 tablespoons of butter.

7. Set your air fryer to 325°F. Place the muffin cups or cake pan into the basket. Cook for 12 minutes, and check for doneness. Cook for up to 3 minutes more, until golden brown.

Cooking tip: Mix the dry ingredients ahead of time. Often, I'll make three or four batches and store them in labeled zip-top bags. This makes throwing this recipe together a cinch!

PER SERVING: Total calories: 227; Total fat: 19g; Total carbohydrates: 7g; Fiber: 3g; Erythritol: 0g; Net carbs: 4g; Protein: 7g

MACROS: 75% Fat; 12% Protein; 13% Carbs

Veggie Frittata

PREP TIME: **7 MINUTES** | COOK TIME: **21 TO 23 MINUTES** | TEMPERATURE: **350°F**

Looking for a fast and easy breakfast that is sure to impress? You will love this Veggie Frittata! This recipe is highly adaptable, so feel free to play with it, using whatever vegetables you have on hand. Frittatas are the perfect recipe to clean out your crisper drawer. I also like to vary the cheeses, subbing in feta or Parmesan for the Cheddar (or if I'm feeling fancy, I'll use all three).   **SERVES 2**

QUICK

KID-FRIENDLY

VEGETARIAN

Avocado oil spray

¼ cup diced red onion

¼ cup diced red bell pepper

¼ cup finely chopped broccoli

4 large eggs

3 ounces shredded sharp Cheddar cheese, divided

½ teaspoon dried thyme

Sea salt

Freshly ground black pepper

1. Spray a 7-inch pan well with oil. Put the onion, pepper, and broccoli in the pan, place the pan in the air fryer, and set to 350°F. Cook for 5 minutes.

2. While the vegetables cook, beat the eggs in a medium bowl. Stir in half of the cheese, and season with the thyme, salt, and pepper.

3. Add the eggs to the pan and top with the remaining cheese. Set the air fryer to 350°F. Cook for 16 to 18 minutes, until cooked through.

Air Fryer tip: If you have a small air fryer and need to use a smaller pan, make sure that it is deep enough to accommodate the eggs. They will expand quite a bit as they cook.

PER SERVING: Total calories: 325; Total fat: 23g; Total carbohydrates: 6g; Fiber: 1g; Erythritol: 0g; Net carbs: 5g; Protein: 22g

MACROS: 64% Fat; 27% Protein; 9% Carbs

Blueberry Muffins

PREP TIME: **10 MINUTES** | COOK TIME: **15 TO 18 MINUTES** | TEMPERATURE: **300°F**

I grew up eating muffins from a box mix, and even so, they were always such a treat. These muffins, which I now make from scratch with keto-friendly ingredients, take me straight back to childhood. **SERVES 6**

QUICK

KID-FRIENDLY

VEGETARIAN

1 cup finely ground blanched almond flour

⅓ cup Swerve Confectioners sweetener

1½ teaspoons baking powder

½ teaspoon baking soda

¼ teaspoon sea salt

¼ teaspoon xanthan gum

1 large egg, beaten

½ cup sour cream

2 tablespoons heavy (whipping) cream

1 teaspoon pure vanilla extract

½ cup fresh or frozen blueberries

Almond Glaze (page 162, optional)

1. In a large bowl, combine the almond flour, Swerve, baking powder, baking soda, sea salt, and xanthan gum.

2. In a medium bowl, whisk together the egg, sour cream, heavy cream, and vanilla.

3. Add the wet ingredients to the dry ingredients, and stir until just combined. Gently stir in the blueberries.

4. Divide the batter among 6 silicone muffin cups or the cups of a muffin pan that fits into your air fryer. Place in the air fryer basket and set to 300°F. Cook for 15 to 18 minutes, until the tops are golden brown and a toothpick inserted into the center appears clean when removed.

5. Drizzle with the almond glaze (if using) before serving.

Air Fryer tip: These muffins tend to brown on top very quickly. Keep a close eye on them.

PER SERVING: Total calories: 194; Total fat: 16g; Total carbohydrates: 19g; Fiber: 2g; Erythritol: 11g; Net carbs: 6g; Protein: 6g

MACROS: 74% Fat; 12% Protein; 14% Carbs

Bacon and Spinach Egg Muffins

PREP TIME: **7 MINUTES** | COOK TIME: **12 TO 14 MINUTES** | TEMPERATURE: **300°F**

When you need a breakfast that you can throw together in a flash, these muffins are perfection. They are great for meal prep, since they can easily be made ahead of time and reheated in your air fryer in just a few minutes. This recipe is another one you can change up, using whatever ingredients you like. I like to add cayenne pepper for a zesty but not-too-spicy edge, but if you're sensitive to spice, feel free to omit it.   **SERVES 6**

QUICK

KID-FRIENDLY

6 large eggs

¼ cup heavy (whipping) cream

½ teaspoon sea salt

¼ teaspoon freshly ground black pepper

¼ teaspoon cayenne pepper (optional)

¾ cup frozen chopped spinach, thawed and drained

4 strips cooked bacon, crumbled

2 ounces shredded Cheddar cheese

1. In a large bowl (with a spout if you have one), whisk together the eggs, heavy cream, salt, black pepper, and cayenne pepper (if using).

2. Divide the spinach and bacon among 6 silicone muffin cups. Place the muffin cups in your air fryer basket.

3. Divide the egg mixture among the muffin cups. Top with the cheese.

4. Set the air fryer to 300°F. Cook for 12 to 14 minutes, until the eggs are set and cooked through.

Variation tip: Broccoli, red bell pepper, arugula, chard, and even jalapeños are all great here. Just add them to the muffin cups instead of the spinach.

PER SERVING: Total calories: 180; Total fat: 14g; Total carbohydrates: 2g; Fiber: 1g; Erythritol: 0g; Net carbs: 1g; Protein: 11g

MACROS: 70% Fat; 24% Protein; 6% Carbs

Smoky Sausage Patties

PREP TIME: **10 MINUTES, PLUS 30 MINUTES TO CHILL** | COOK TIME: **9 MINUTES** | TEMPERATURE: **400°F**

Sure, you can buy breakfast sausage, but homemade tastes so much better. These patties are fabulous by themselves, on an egg sandwich, or with a fried egg. They're also great to make ahead of time and freeze until needed. Just reheat the patties in your air fryer when you're ready to enjoy them. **SERVES 8**

KID-FRIENDLY

1 pound ground pork

1 tablespoon coconut aminos

2 teaspoons liquid smoke

1 teaspoon dried sage

1 teaspoon sea salt

½ teaspoon fennel seeds

½ teaspoon dried thyme

½ teaspoon freshly ground black pepper

¼ teaspoon cayenne pepper

1. In a large bowl, combine the pork, coconut aminos, liquid smoke, sage, salt, fennel seeds, thyme, black pepper, and cayenne pepper. Work the meat with your hands until the seasonings are fully incorporated.

2. Shape the mixture into 8 equal-size patties. Using your thumb, make a dent in the center of each patty. Place the patties on a plate and cover with plastic wrap. Refrigerate the patties for at least 30 minutes.

3. Working in batches if necessary, place the patties in a single layer in the air fryer, being careful not to overcrowd them.

4. Set the air fryer to 400°F and cook for 5 minutes. Flip and cook for about 4 minutes more.

Substitution tip: Ground chicken or turkey may be used in place of the ground pork.

PER SERVING: Total calories: 152; Total fat: 12g; Total carbohydrates: 1g; Fiber: 0g; Erythritol: 0g; Net carbs: 1g; Protein: 10g

MACROS: 71% Fat; 26% Protein; 3% Carbs

Buffalo Chicken Breakfast Muffins

PREP TIME: **7 MINUTES** | COOK TIME: **13 TO 16 MINUTES** | TEMPERATURE: **300°F**

With three kids and a business, it is recipes like this that keep me sane! I like to make a double batch of breakfast muffins over the weekend so everyone in the family can have grab-and-go breakfasts during the week ahead. **SERVES 10**

QUICK

FAVORITE

6 ounces shredded cooked chicken

3 ounces blue cheese, crumbled

2 tablespoons unsalted butter, melted

⅓ cup Buffalo hot sauce, such as Frank's RedHot

1 teaspoon minced garlic

6 large eggs

Sea salt

Freshly ground black pepper

Avocado oil spray

1. In a large bowl, stir together the chicken, blue cheese, melted butter, hot sauce, and garlic.

2. In a medium bowl or large liquid measuring cup, beat the eggs. Season with salt and pepper.

3. Spray 10 silicone muffin cups with oil. Divide the chicken mixture among the cups, and pour the egg mixture over top.

4. Place the cups in the air fryer and set to 300°F. Cook for 13 to 16 minutes, until the muffins are set and cooked through. (Depending on the size of your air fryer, you may need to cook the muffins in batches.)

Substitution tip: I love blue cheese any time of day, but for some people, it is too much first thing in the morning. Feel free to substitute another cheese if you like. Cheddar is great here.

PER SERVING: Total calories: 120; Total fat: 8g; Total carbohydrates: 1g; Fiber: 0g; Erythritol: 0g; Net carbs: 1g; Protein: 9g

MACROS: 60% Fat; 30% Protein; 10% Carbs

Radish Home Fries

PREP TIME: **10 MINUTES** | COOK TIME: **16 MINUTES** | AIR FRYER TEMPERATURE: **350°F, THEN 400°F**

I came up with this recipe on a weekend morning when I was missing potatoes for breakfast. You may not think that peppery-hot radishes would make a good substitute for potatoes, but give it a try. Cooking radishes changes them, replacing their pungency with sweetness. This recipe nods to traditional home fries in flavor, but with keto-friendly ingredients. It's a perfect choice for those days when you are craving comfort food.　**SERVES 4**

QUICK

VEGETARIAN

1½ cups coarsely chopped radishes

½ cup chopped onion

1 jalapeño, seeded and diced

1 teaspoon garlic powder

½ teaspoon smoked paprika

Sea salt

Freshly ground black pepper

1 tablespoon avocado oil

2 tablespoons chopped fresh cilantro or parsley, for garnish

1. Place the radishes in a deep air fryer–safe pot and add the onion, jalapeño, garlic powder, and paprika. Season to taste with salt and pepper. Drizzle the oil over top of the mixture and toss to coat.

2. Set the air fryer to 350°F and cook for 8 minutes.

3. After 8 minutes, increase the temperature to 400°F, then cook for another 8 minutes.

4. Garnish with cilantro or parsley. Serve warm.

Variation tip: Feel free to experiment with the add-ins here. Sometimes I like to use shallots in place of the onion and jalapeño, and top the vegetables with fresh chives and a dollop of sour cream.

PER SERVING: Total calories: 52; Total fat: 4g; Total carbohydrates: 4g; Fiber: 1g; Erythritol: 0g; Net carbs: 3g; Protein: 1g

MACROS: 69% Fat; 8% Protein; 23% Carbs

Classic Egg Sandwich

PREP TIME: **10 MINUTES** | COOK TIME: **12 TO 14 MINUTES** | TEMPERATURE: **300°F**

My youngest son's favorite breakfast is an egg sandwich, and I love that I can make him one in the air fryer with little hands-on time and without heating my stove or oven. For heartier appetites, the addition of bacon or sausage is nice here. **SERVES 1**

QUICK

KID-FRIENDLY

VEGETARIAN

Avocado oil spray

1 large egg

Sea salt

Freshly ground black pepper

2 tablespoons unsalted butter, at room temperature

2 slices keto-friendly bread (or Down Home Biscuits, page 22)

2 slices Cheddar cheese

¼ avocado, sliced

Hot sauce, for serving

1. Line a small air fryer–safe cake pan with parchment paper. Spray a 3½-inch egg ring with oil, then place it in the prepared pan.

2. Place the pan in the air fryer and set to 300°F. Let preheat for 5 minutes.

3. Once the air fryer is preheated, crack an egg into the egg ring. Season with salt and pepper. Cook for 6 to 8 minutes, until the egg is set. Remove from the pan.

4. Spread the butter on one side of each bread slice and place them in the pan. Cook for 4 minutes, or until the butter is melted and the bread is lightly toasted.

5. Place the egg on one of the toasted bread slices, and top with the cheese slices. Cook until the cheese melts, about 2 minutes.

6. Top with the avocado and hot sauce, place the second bread slice on top, and serve.

Cooking tip: If you plan on using the Down Home Biscuits (page 22) to make the egg sandwiches, make sure you use a smaller egg ring so that you don't end up with more egg than bread!

PER SERVING (WITH 1 DOWN HOME BISCUIT): Total calories: 735; Total fat: 66g; Total carbohydrates: 11g; Fiber: 6g; Erythritol: 0g; Net carbs: 5g; Protein: 24g

MACROS: 80% Fat; 13% Protein; 6% Carbs

Southwestern Breakfast Taco

PREP TIME: 10 MINUTES | **COOK TIME: 9 MINUTES** | **TEMPERATURE: 400°F**

If you are familiar with the chaffle craze—waffles made from egg and cheese—then you know it is entirely possible to make a keto-friendly bread substitute. When you cook the egg-and-cheese mixture in the air fryer, it doesn't get as crispy as it does in a waffle maker. Instead, it is soft and pliable—the perfect substitute for a wrap or soft taco. **SERVES 1**

QUICK

1 large egg, beaten

½ cup shredded mozzarella cheese

1 tablespoon finely ground blanched almond flour

1 tablespoon canned chopped green chiles

1 teaspoon Taco Seasoning (page 167)

½ teaspoon baking powder

2 strips cooked bacon, crumbled

¼ avocado, diced

2 tablespoons shredded Cheddar cheese

2 tablespoons sour cream

1 tablespoon salsa

Chopped fresh cilantro, for serving (optional)

Hot sauce, for serving (optional)

1. In a medium bowl, whisk together the egg, mozzarella cheese, almond flour, chiles, taco seasoning, and baking powder.

2. Line a 7-inch air fryer–safe baking pan with parchment paper. Spread the egg-cheese mixture in an even layer in the prepared pan. Place the pan in the air fryer basket and set to 400°F. Cook for 9 minutes or until the mixture is set.

3. Remove from the pan and top with the bacon, avocado, Cheddar cheese, sour cream, and salsa.

4. Serve warm with cilantro and hot sauce (if using).

PER SERVING: Total calories: 563; Total fat: 42g; Total carbohydrates: 11g; Fiber: 5g; Erythritol: 0g; Net carbs: 6g; Protein: 34g

MACROS: 67% Fat; 24% Protein; 9% Carbs

Spinach and Feta Egg Bake

PREP TIME: **7 MINUTES** | COOK TIME: **23 TO 25 MINUTES** | TEMPERATURE: **350°F**

This easy egg bake deserves to become part of your regular cooking routine. It is one of my favorite ways to work some veggies into my family's breakfast. If you are cooking for one, you can store leftovers for up to 2 days in the refrigerator and reheat them in the oven or microwave—or simply pop it back in the air fryer for 5 to 7 minutes at 350°F. **SERVES 2**

VEGETARIAN

Avocado oil spray

⅓ cup diced red onion

1 cup frozen chopped spinach, thawed and drained

4 large eggs

¼ cup heavy (whipping) cream

Sea salt

Freshly ground black pepper

¼ teaspoon cayenne pepper

½ cup crumbled feta cheese

¼ cup shredded Parmesan cheese

1. Spray a deep 7-inch air fryer–safe pan with oil. Put the onion in the pan, and place the pan in the air fryer basket. Set the air fryer to 350°F and cook for 7 minutes.

2. Sprinkle the spinach over the onion.

3. In a medium bowl, beat the eggs, heavy cream, salt, black pepper, and cayenne. Pour this mixture over the vegetables.

4. Top with the feta and Parmesan cheese. Cook for 16 to 18 minutes, until the eggs are set and lightly brown.

Variation tip: I love the simplicity of this recipe, but now and then I like to jazz it up. Great additions include chopped olives, diced roasted red peppers, and shredded cooked chicken. Or try adding bacon and using goat cheese in place of the feta. This recipe is infinitely adaptable, so have fun with it.

PER SERVING: Total calories: 424; Total fat: 32g; Total carbohydrates: 11g; Fiber: 3g; Erythritol: 0g; Net carbs: 8g; Protein: 26g

MACROS: 68% Fat; 25% Protein; 7% Carbs

Bacon-Wrapped Jalapeño
Poppers, page 42

3

Sides & Snacks

Buffalo Cauliflower Wings

PREP TIME: **20 MINUTES** | COOK TIME: **10 TO 12 MINUTES** | TEMPERATURE: **400°F**

People go crazy over these wings! When I first created this recipe, I made it three days in a row at my family's request. The buttery, tangy sauce paired with surprisingly crispy cauliflower makes the taste buds sing. Serve these "wings" as a side dish paired with something simple, such as Fried Chicken Breasts (page 56). **SERVES 6**

VEGETARIAN

FAVORITE

- 1 head cauliflower
- 3 large eggs
- ¾ cup finely ground blanched almond flour
- ¾ cup finely grated Parmesan cheese
- 1 teaspoon garlic powder
- ½ teaspoon smoked paprika
- ½ teaspoon sea salt
- ½ teaspoon freshly ground black pepper
- Avocado oil spray
- 1 cup Buffalo hot sauce, such as Frank's RedHot
- 4 tablespoons unsalted butter
- Garlic Ranch Dressing (page 168) or Blue Cheese Dressing (page 169), for serving

1. Line a baking sheet or platter with parchment paper.

2. Core the cauliflower and cut it into large florets.

3. Beat the eggs together in a small bowl. In a separate bowl, combine the almond flour, Parmesan, garlic powder, smoked paprika, salt, and pepper.

4. Dip a cauliflower floret into the egg, then coat it in the almond flour mixture, making sure to firmly press the mixture into the cauliflower. Transfer the coated floret to the prepared baking sheet. Continue with the remaining cauliflower, egg, and almond flour mixture.

5. Set the air fryer to 400°F. Spray the cauliflower with oil. Place the florets in the air fryer basket in a single layer, working in batches if necessary, and cook for 5 minutes. Flip the florets and spray them with more oil. Continue cooking for 5 to 7 minutes more.

6. While the cauliflower is cooking, make the sauce. Place the hot sauce and butter in a small saucepan over medium-low heat. Heat, stirring occasionally, until the butter melts.

7. Toss the crispy cauliflower in the sauce, then use a slotted spoon to transfer the coated cauliflower to a plate or platter. Serve warm with the dressing.

Cooking tip: Leftover Buffalo cauliflower can be surprisingly good if you reheat it in your air fryer. Reheat the cauliflower at 400°F for 5 to 7 minutes or until heated through.

PER SERVING: Total calories: 306; Total fat: 21g; Total carbohydrates: 9g; Fiber: 4g; Erythritol: 0g; Net carbs: 5g; Protein: 13g

MACROS: 62% Fat; 17% Protein; 21% Carbs

Smoky Zucchini Chips

PREP TIME: **15 MINUTES** | COOK TIME: **8 TO 10 MINUTES** | TEMPERATURE: **400°F**

I am wild about these chips, and I think you will be, too. Crispy on the outside and tender on the inside, these delicious nibbles are loved by all (even those not on a low-carb diet). They are perfect for game day or any time you need something to serve as a vessel for a delicious dip, such as Garlic Ranch Dressing (page 168) or Blue Cheese Dressing (page 169)—that is most definitely a real *need* at times.   SERVES 6

QUICK

KID-FRIENDLY

VEGETARIAN

2 large eggs

1 cup finely ground blanched almond flour

½ cup Parmesan cheese

1½ teaspoons sea salt

1 teaspoon garlic powder

½ teaspoon smoked paprika

¼ teaspoon freshly ground black pepper

2 zucchini, cut into ¼-inch-thick slices

Avocado oil spray

1. Beat the eggs in a shallow bowl. In another bowl, stir together the almond flour, Parmesan cheese, salt, garlic powder, smoked paprika, and black pepper.

2. Dip the zucchini slices in the egg mixture, then coat them with the almond flour mixture.

3. Set the air fryer to 400°F. Place the zucchini chips in a single layer in the air fryer basket, working in batches if necessary. Spray the chips with oil and cook for 4 minutes. Flip the chips and spray them with more oil. Cook for 4 to 6 minutes more.

4. Serve with your favorite dipping sauce.

PER SERVING: Total calories: 181; Total fat: 14g; Total carbohydrates: 7g; Fiber: 3g; Erythritol: 0g; Net carbs: 4g; Protein: 11g

MACROS: 70% Fat; 24% Protein; 6% Carbs

Lemon-Garlic Mushrooms

PREP TIME: **10 MINUTES** | COOK TIME: **10 TO 15 MINUTES** | TEMPERATURE: **375°F**

Mushrooms are my forever go-to favorite when it comes to adding a little something extra to steaks, burgers, chicken, pizza, or a wrap. They are the perfect way to boost flavor and earthiness without additional carbs. It doesn't get much better than these perfectly air-fried mushrooms in a lemon-garlic butter sauce; they ensure dinnertime bliss.   **SERVES 6**

QUICK

VEGETARIAN

FAVORITE

12 ounces sliced mushrooms

1 tablespoon avocado oil

Sea salt

Freshly ground black pepper

3 tablespoons unsalted butter

1 teaspoon minced garlic

1 teaspoon freshly squeezed lemon juice

½ teaspoon red pepper flakes

2 tablespoons chopped fresh parsley

1. Place the mushrooms in a medium bowl and toss with the oil. Season to taste with salt and pepper.

2. Place the mushrooms in a single layer in the air fryer basket. Set your air fryer to 375°F and cook for 10 to 15 minutes, until the mushrooms are tender.

3. While the mushrooms cook, melt the butter in a small pot or skillet over medium-low heat. Stir in the garlic and cook for 30 seconds. Remove the pot from the heat and stir in the lemon juice and red pepper flakes.

4. Toss the mushrooms with the lemon-garlic butter and garnish with the parsley before serving.

Variation tip: Sometimes I like to mix up the seasonings by adding a teaspoon of dried basil and a tablespoon of white cooking wine to the butter mixture. Rosemary is also an excellent addition—especially if you are preparing this to serve over steak.

PER SERVING: Total calories: 80; Total fat: 8g; Total carbohydrates: 1g; Fiber: <1g; Erythritol: 0g; Net carbs: 1g; Protein: 1g

MACROS: 90% Fat; 5% Protein; 5% Carbs

Sweet and Spicy Pecans

PREP TIME: **7 MINUTES** | COOK TIME: **15 MINUTES** | TEMPERATURE: **275°F**

These pecans make an incredible low-carb snack and are also a fabulous addition to salad. They are so popular in my house that I have to hide them if I want them to last more than a few days. I always wish I'd doubled the recipe! **SERVES 8**

QUICK

KID-FRIENDLY

VEGETARIAN

FAVORITE

5-INGREDIENT

3 tablespoons unsalted butter, melted

¼ cup brown sugar substitute, such as Swerve or Sukrin Gold

1½ teaspoons Maldon sea salt (or regular sea salt if you like)

¼ teaspoon cayenne pepper, more or less to taste

2 cups pecan halves

1. Line your air fryer basket with parchment paper or an air fryer liner.

2. Place the melted butter in a small pot and whisk in the brown sugar substitute, sea salt, and cayenne pepper. Stir until well combined.

3. Place the pecans in a medium bowl and pour the butter mixture over them. Toss to coat.

4. Set the air fryer to 275°F. Place the pecans in the air fryer basket in a single layer, working in batches if necessary, and cook for 10 minutes. Stir, then cook for 5 minutes more.

5. Transfer the pecans to a parchment paper–lined baking sheet and allow them to cool completely before serving. Store them in an airtight container at room temperature for up to 1 week.

Substitution tip: If you don't have brown sugar substitute on hand, any keto-friendly sweetener will work here instead.

PER SERVING: Total calories: 225; Total fat: 24g; Total carbohydrates: 10g; Fiber: 3g; Erythritol: 6g; Net carbs: 1g; Protein: 3g

MACROS: 96% Fat; 4% Protein; 0% Carbs

Roasted Brussels Sprouts with Bacon

PREP TIME: **10 MINUTES** | COOK TIME: **15 TO 18 MINUTES** | TEMPERATURE: **375°F**

If you think you don't love Brussels sprouts, this dish might just change your mind. These smoky sprouts are crispy on the outside and perfectly tender on the inside. I like to serve them with a side of Sriracha Mayonnaise (page 165). **SERVES 6**

QUICK

1 pound Brussels sprouts, trimmed and halved

1 tablespoon avocado oil

1 tablespoon coconut aminos

1 teaspoon garlic powder

1 teaspoon smoked paprika

Sea salt

Freshly ground black pepper

4 strips cooked bacon, crumbled

1. Place the Brussels sprouts in a large bowl and toss them with the avocado oil, coconut aminos, garlic powder, smoked paprika, salt, and pepper.

2. Set the air fryer to 375°F and arrange the Brussels sprouts in a single layer in the air fryer basket, working in batches if necessary.

3. Cook for 15 to 18 minutes, stirring halfway through, until the sprouts are brown and crispy.

4. Transfer the sprouts to a bowl and toss with the bacon. Serve warm.

Cooking tip: If you are short on time, you can often find trimmed and halved Brussels sprouts in the prepared foods section of your grocery store's produce department. Make sure you check out page 177 to learn tips and tricks for cooking bacon in the air fryer. If you want to take the flavor to the next level, cook the bacon in a clean air fryer, then remove the bacon grease from the pan and use it in place of the avocado oil.

PER SERVING: Total calories: 89; Total fat: 5g; Total carbohydrates: 8g; Fiber: 3g; Erythritol: 0g; Net carbs: 5g; Protein: 11g

MACROS: 70% Fat; 24% Protein; 6% Carbs

Bacon-Wrapped Jalapeño Poppers

PREP TIME: **15 MINUTES** | COOK TIME: **17 TO 22 MINUTES** | TEMPERATURE: **400°F**

I've always loved deep-fried jalapeño poppers, and I was delighted to find that they taste just as good without the breading. These keto poppers are a game-changer. They pack a ton of flavor without requiring too many ingredients. This is an appetizer that you will be proud to serve to friends and family.   SERVES 12

FAVORITE

12 jalapeño peppers

8 ounces cream cheese, at room temperature

2 tablespoons minced onion

1 teaspoon garlic powder

½ teaspoon smoked paprika

Sea salt

Freshly ground black pepper

12 strips bacon

1. Slice the jalapeños in half lengthwise, then seed them and remove any remaining white membranes to make room for the filling. Set the air fryer to 400°F. Place the jalapeños in a single layer, cut-side down, in the air fryer basket. Cook for 7 minutes.

2. Remove the peppers from the air fryer and place them on a paper towel, cut-side up. Allow them to rest until they are cool enough to handle.

3. While the jalapeños are cooking, in a medium bowl, stir together the cream cheese, minced onion, garlic powder, and smoked paprika. Season to taste with salt and pepper.

4. Spoon the cream cheese filling into the jalapeños.

5. Cut the bacon strips in half, and wrap 1 piece around each stuffed jalapeño half.

6. Place the bacon-wrapped jalapeños, cut-side up, in a single layer in the air fryer basket. Cook for 10 to 15 minutes, until the bacon is crispy.

PER SERVING: Total calories: 116; Total fat: 10g; Total carbohydrates: 2g; Fiber: 1g; Erythritol: 0g; Net carbs: 1g; Protein: 4g

MACROS: 78% Fat; 21% Protein; 1% Carbs

Everything Kale Chips

PREP TIME: **10 MINUTES** | COOK TIME: **10 TO 14 MINUTES** | TEMPERATURE: **325°F**

If you love snacks that practically cook themselves, you are going to go crazy for these kale chips. I have loved kale chips for years but have always found them too fussy to make at home. The air fryer makes them quick and easy—you don't even have to worry about arranging them in a single layer. **SERVES 8**

QUICK

VEGETARIAN

5-INGREDIENT

1 bunch kale, washed, stemmed, and torn into pieces

1 tablespoon extra-virgin olive oil

2 teaspoons everything seasoning (see Ingredient Tip)

1. Place the kale leaves in a large bowl. Toss with the olive oil and seasoning.

2. Arrange half of the kale in the air fryer basket. Set the air fryer to 325°F. Cook for 5 to 7 minutes, shaking halfway through, until the kale is crispy. Repeat with the remaining kale.

Cooking tip: Because kale chips are so light, they are going to blow around a bit in the air fryer. When you are done cooking, allow the air fryer to cool. Unplug it, then carefully wipe a paper towel over the heating element to make sure there aren't any stray kale chips stuck to it.

Ingredient tip: Everything seasoning is available in most supermarkets or online, but it's also very easy to make it yourself. Just combine 1 tablespoon each of poppy seeds, dried minced garlic, dried minced onion, and sesame seeds, and 2 teaspoons of sea salt. I like to sprinkle it on eggs, spiced nuts, and cheese straws.

PER SERVING: Total calories: 35; Total fat: 2g; Total carbohydrates: 3g; Fiber: 1g; Erythritol: 0g; Net carbs: 2g; Protein: 1g

MACROS: 51% Fat; 11% Protein; 38% Carbs

Onion Rings

PREP TIME: **15 MINUTES** | COOK TIME: **10 MINUTES** | TEMPERATURE: **350°F**

Onion rings are my favorite when it comes to appetizers. You will be amazed at how much like the "real thing" this keto-friendly version is. If you are tracking macros, this is a recipe you will want to enjoy in moderation, since onions are a bit high in carbs. To me, it's a worthy indulgence. Serve these with Garlic Ranch Dressing (page 168) or Blue Cheese Dressing (page 169).   **SERVES 6**

QUICK

VEGETARIAN

FAVORITE

1 large sweet onion

1 cup finely ground blanched almond flour

1 cup finely grated Parmesan cheese

1 tablespoon baking powder

1 teaspoon smoked paprika

Sea salt

Freshly ground black pepper

2 large eggs

1 tablespoon heavy (whipping) cream

Avocado oil spray

1. Cut the onion crosswise into ⅓-inch-thick rings.

2. In a medium bowl, combine the almond flour, Parmesan cheese, baking powder, smoked paprika, and salt and pepper to taste.

3. In a separate medium bowl, beat the eggs and heavy cream together.

4. Dip an onion ring in the egg mixture and then into the almond flour mixture. Press the almond flour mixture into the onion. Transfer to a parchment paper–lined baking sheet (I find the parchment helps reduce sticking during prep) and repeat with the remaining onion slices.

5. Set the air fryer to 350°F. Arrange the onion rings in a single layer in the air fryer basket, working in batches if needed. Spray the onion rings with oil and cook for 5 minutes.

6. Use a spatula to carefully reach under the onions and flip them. Spray the onion rings with oil again and cook for 5 minutes more.

Cooking tip: Don't skip pressing the almond flour mixture into the onions. It needs to be firmly adhered to the surface, or the air fryer will blow the breading off. If you don't have baking powder, you can make your own by combining one part baking soda with two parts cream of tartar.

PER SERVING: Total calories: 220; Total fat: 14g; Total carbohydrates: 10g; Fiber: 3g; Erythritol: 0g; Net carbs: 7g; Protein: 14g

MACROS: 57% Fat; 25% Protein; 18% Carbs

Cabbage Wedges with Caraway Butter

PREP TIME: **15 MINUTES, PLUS 20 MINUTES TO 1 HOUR TO CHILL THE BUTTER** | COOK TIME: **35 TO 40 MINUTES** | TEMPERATURE: **375°F**

I think cabbage is an underappreciated vegetable. In this recipe, cabbage wedges are air fried until they're crispy on the outside and tender on the inside. Caraway seeds add a lovely, earthy flavor. **SERVES 6**

VEGETARIAN

5-INGREDIENT

1 tablespoon caraway seeds

½ cup (1 stick) unsalted butter, at room temperature

½ teaspoon grated lemon zest

1 small head green or red cabbage, cut into 6 wedges

1 tablespoon avocado oil

½ teaspoon sea salt

¼ teaspoon freshly ground black pepper

1. Place the caraway seeds in a small dry skillet over medium-high heat. Toast the seeds for 2 to 3 minutes, then remove them from the heat and let cool. Lightly crush the seeds using a mortar and pestle or with the back of a knife.

2. Place the butter in a small bowl and stir in the crushed caraway seeds and lemon zest. Form the butter into a log and wrap it in parchment paper or plastic wrap. Refrigerate for at least 1 hour or freeze for 20 minutes.

3. Brush or spray the cabbage wedges with the avocado oil, and sprinkle with the salt and pepper.

4. Set the air fryer to 375°F. Place the cabbage in a single layer in the air fryer basket and cook for 20 minutes. Flip and cook for 15 to 20 minutes more, until the cabbage is tender and lightly charred.

5. Plate the cabbage and dot with caraway butter. Tent with foil for 5 minutes to melt the butter, and serve.

PER SERVING: Total calories: 191; Total fat: 18g; Total carbohydrates: 7g; Fiber: 3g; Erythritol: 0g; Net carbs: 4g; Protein: 2g

MACROS: 85% Fat; 2% Protein; 13% Carbs

Garlic-Parmesan Jícama Fries

PREP TIME: **10 MINUTES** | COOK TIME: **25 TO 35 MINUTES** | TEMPERATURE: **400°F**

If you have never had jícama before, you are in for such a treat. When raw, it tastes like a cross between celery root and apple, but when you fry it, it turns into a perfect French fry substitute. I love the garlic-Parmesan sauce here, but they are also great simply salted and served with keto-friendly ketchup. **SERVES 4**

KID-FRIENDLY

VEGETARIAN

FAVORITE

1 medium jícama, peeled

1 tablespoon avocado oil

¼ cup (4 tablespoons) unsalted butter

1 tablespoon minced garlic

¾ teaspoon chopped dried rosemary

¾ teaspoon sea salt

½ teaspoon freshly ground black pepper

⅓ cup grated Parmesan cheese

Chopped fresh parsley, for garnish

Maldon sea salt, for garnish

1. Using a spiralizer or julienne peeler, cut the jícama into shoestrings, then cut them into 3-inch-long sticks.

2. Bring a large pot of water to boil. Add the jícama and cook for about 10 minutes. Drain and dry on paper towels. Transfer to a medium bowl and toss with the oil.

3. Set the air fryer to 400°F. Arrange the jícama in a single layer in the basket, working in batches if necessary. Cook for 15 to 25 minutes, checking at intervals, until tender and golden brown.

4. While the fries cook, melt the butter over medium-high heat. Add the garlic, rosemary, salt, and pepper. Cook for about 1 minute.

5. Toss the fries with the garlic butter. Top with the Parmesan cheese, and sprinkle with parsley and Maldon sea salt.

PER SERVING: Total calories: 239; Total fat: 18g; Total carbohydrates: 16g; Fiber: 8g; Erythritol: 0g; Net carbs: 8g; Protein: 5g

MACROS: 68% Fat; 8% Protein; 24% Carbs

Lemon-Thyme Asparagus

PREP TIME: **5 MINUTES** | COOK TIME: **4 TO 8 MINUTES** | TEMPERATURE: **400°F**

This fast and easy recipe is one I turn to again and again. Here, perfectly cooked crisp-tender asparagus gets the addition of fragrant thyme, then a zippy topping of lemon juice, lemon zest, and creamy goat cheese. This is a tried-and-true weeknight staple.   SERVES 4

QUICK

VEGETARIAN

- **1 pound asparagus, woody ends trimmed off**
- **1 tablespoon avocado oil**
- **½ teaspoon dried thyme or ½ tablespoon chopped fresh thyme**
- **Sea salt**
- **Freshly ground black pepper**
- **2 ounces goat cheese, crumbled**
- **Zest and juice of 1 lemon**
- **Flaky sea salt, for serving (optional)**

1. In a medium bowl, toss together the asparagus, avocado oil, and thyme, and season with sea salt and pepper.

2. Place the asparagus in the air fryer basket in a single layer. Set the air fryer to 400°F and cook for 4 to 8 minutes, to your desired doneness (see Cooking tip).

3. Transfer to a serving platter. Top with the goat cheese, lemon zest, and lemon juice. If desired, season with a pinch of flaky salt.

Cooking tip: I like my asparagus firm, so I tend to cook it for about 4 minutes. If you prefer softer asparagus or want it lightly charred, you will want to cook it for closer to 8 minutes.

PER SERVING: Total calories: 103; Total fat: 7g; Total carbohydrates: 7g; Fiber: 3g; Erythritol: 0g; Net carbs: 4g; Protein: 5g

MACROS: 61% Fat; 19% Protein; 20% Carbs

Parmesan-Rosemary Radishes

PREP TIME: **5 MINUTES** | COOK TIME: **15 TO 20 MINUTES** | TEMPERATURE: **375°F**

While I appreciate raw radishes in moderation, I am obsessed with the mild sweetness that comes from roasting them. These delicious morsels once again take the place of roasted potatoes, while remaining uniquely delicious on their own. Whatever you do, don't skip the cheese here—it is the star of the show.   **SERVES 4**

QUICK

KID-FRIENDLY

VEGETARIAN

5-INGREDIENT

1 bunch radishes, stemmed, trimmed, and quartered

1 tablespoon avocado oil

2 tablespoons finely grated fresh Parmesan cheese

1 tablespoon chopped fresh rosemary

Sea salt

Freshly ground black pepper

1. Place the radishes in a medium bowl and toss them with the avocado oil, Parmesan cheese, rosemary, salt, and pepper.

2. Set the air fryer to 375°F. Arrange the radishes in a single layer in the air fryer basket. Cook for 15 to 20 minutes, until golden brown and tender. Let cool for 5 minutes before serving.

Ingredient tip: I like common round radishes here, which are sometimes labeled "Easter egg radishes." If you like, diced daikon radishes will also work.

PER SERVING: Total calories: 47; Total fat: 4g; Total carbohydrates: 1g; Fiber: <1g; Erythritol: 0g; Net carbs: 1g; Protein: 1g

MACROS: 77% Fat; 9% Protein; 14% Carbs

Spicy Roasted Broccoli

PREP TIME: **8 MINUTES** | COOK TIME: **10 TO 14 MINUTES** | TEMPERATURE: **375°F**

Fast and healthy sides are a must when you want to stay on track with your health goals. This broccoli dish has just the right amount of punch from the garlic and red pepper flakes, while lemon juice and zest keep the flavors perky and bright. If you are pressed for time, pre-minced garlic and pre-cut broccoli florets make this recipe even easier.   SERVES 6

QUICK

VEGETARIAN

5-INGREDIENT

1 head broccoli, cut into bite-size florets

1 tablespoon avocado oil

2 teaspoons minced garlic

⅛ teaspoon red pepper flakes

Sea salt

Freshly ground black pepper

1 tablespoon freshly squeezed lemon juice

½ teaspoon lemon zest

1. In a large bowl, toss together the broccoli, avocado oil, garlic, red pepper flakes, salt, and pepper.

2. Set the air fryer to 375°F. Arrange the broccoli in a single layer in the air fryer basket, working in batches if necessary. Cook for 10 to 14 minutes, until the broccoli is lightly charred.

3. Place the florets in a medium bowl and toss with the lemon juice and lemon zest. Serve.

Cooking tip: Feel free to use the broccoli stalks here, too. Trim off the leaves, cut the stems into cubes, and toss them with the florets.

PER SERVING: Total calories: 52; Total fat: 3g; Total carbohydrates: 6g; Fiber: 3g; Erythritol: 0g; Net carbs: 3g; Protein: 3g

MACROS: 52% Fat; 23% Protein; 25% Carbs

Buttery Green Beans

PREP TIME: **5 MINUTES** | COOK TIME: **8 TO 10 MINUTES** | TEMPERATURE: **400°F**

Fresh green beans are the perfect pairing for the deep saltiness of Parmesan cheese. If you like to add a little extra something to your veggies, I suggest topping the cooked beans with a squeeze of fresh lemon juice and a sprinkle of red pepper flakes. **SERVES 6**

QUICK

KID-FRIENDLY

VEGETARIAN

5-INGREDIENT

1 pound green beans, trimmed

1 tablespoon avocado oil

1 teaspoon garlic powder

Sea salt

Freshly ground black pepper

¼ cup (4 tablespoons) unsalted butter, melted

¼ cup freshly grated Parmesan cheese

1. In a large bowl, toss together the green beans, avocado oil, and garlic powder and season with salt and pepper.

2. Set the air fryer to 400°F. Arrange the green beans in a single layer in the air fryer basket. Cook for 8 to 10 minutes, tossing halfway through.

3. Transfer the beans to a large bowl and toss with the melted butter. Top with the Parmesan cheese and serve warm.

Variation tip: Feel free to substitute another cheese here. Asiago, blue, feta, and goat cheese all play nicely with green beans.

PER SERVING: Total calories: 134; Total fat: 11g; Total carbohydrates: 6g; Fiber: 3g; Erythritol: 0g; Net carbs: 3g; Protein: 3g

MACROS: 74% Fat; 9% Protein; 17% Carbs

Fried Pickles

PREP TIME: **20 MINUTES, PLUS 20 MINUTES TO FREEZE** | COOK TIME: **10 TO 12 MINUTES** | TEMPERATURE: **400°F**

If you didn't grow up in the South, fried pickles might have you skeptically raising your eyebrows. Trust me—you need these pickles in your life! They make a fun and unique appetizer and are also fabulous with a burger. I like to serve them with Garlic Ranch Dressing (page 168) or Blue Cheese Dressing (page 169). **SERVES 8**

VEGETARIAN

16 ounces whole dill pickles (see Ingredient tip)

2 large eggs, beaten

2 tablespoons heavy (whipping) cream

½ cup finely ground blanched almond flour

½ cup grated Parmesan cheese

1 teaspoon Cajun seasoning

¼ teaspoon cayenne pepper, more or less to taste

Salt

Freshly ground black pepper

Avocado oil spray

1. Cut the pickles in half lengthwise and then cut each half into quarters. Alternatively, you can slice them into rounds.

2. Combine the eggs and heavy cream in a shallow bowl. In a separate bowl, combine the almond flour, Parmesan cheese, Cajun seasoning, cayenne pepper, and salt and black pepper to taste.

3. Dip the pickles in the eggs and then coat them with the almond flour mixture. Press the almond flour mixture firmly into the pickles. Place the coated pickles on a parchment paper–lined baking sheet or platter and freeze for 20 minutes.

4. Preheat the air fryer to 400°F. Spray the pickles with oil and arrange them in a single layer in the air fryer basket, working in batches if necessary. Cook for 6 minutes. Flip the pickles and spray them again with oil. Cook for 4 to 6 minutes more, until they are golden brown.

5. Serve warm with your favorite dipping sauce.

Ingredient tip: In general, pickles are keto-friendly, but you must read the label. Some brands do contain sweeteners, often in the form of high-fructose corn syrup. My go-to brand is Bubbies, which you can find in the refrigerated section of most grocery stores. In addition to being delicious, they are fermented, which is fantastic for your gut health.

PER SERVING: Total calories: 105; Total fat: 8g; Total carbohydrates: 4g; Fiber: 1g; Erythritol: 0g; Net carbs: 3g; Protein: 6g

MACROS: 69% Fat; 23% Protein; 8% Carbs

Turkey Pot Pie, page 72

4

Poultry

Fried Chicken Breasts

PREP TIME: **10 MINUTES, PLUS 2 HOURS TO BRINE** | COOK TIME: **12 TO 14 MINUTES** | TEMPERATURE: **400°F**

Be gone, processed frozen chicken nuggets from a bag! Your family will never guess that this chicken isn't traditionally fried. The marinade keeps the meat moist and tender, and the coating gets perfectly crisp.   SERVES 4

KID-FRIENDLY

FAVORITE

5-INGREDIENT

1 pound boneless, skinless chicken breasts

¾ cup dill pickle juice (see Ingredient tip on page 53)

¾ cup finely ground blanched almond flour

¾ cup finely grated Parmesan cheese

½ teaspoon sea salt

½ teaspoon freshly ground black pepper

2 large eggs

Avocado oil spray

1. Place the chicken breasts in a zip-top bag or between two pieces of plastic wrap. Using a meat mallet or heavy skillet, pound the chicken to a uniform ½-inch thickness.

2. Place the chicken in a large bowl with the pickle juice. Cover and allow to brine in the refrigerator for up to 2 hours.

3. In a shallow dish, combine the almond flour, Parmesan cheese, salt, and pepper. In a separate, shallow bowl, beat the eggs.

4. Drain the chicken and pat it dry with paper towels. Dip in the eggs and then in the flour mixture, making sure to press the coating into the chicken. Spray both sides of the coated breasts with oil.

5. Spray the air fryer basket with oil and put the chicken inside. Set the temperature to 400°F and cook for 6 to 7 minutes.

6. Carefully flip the breasts with a spatula. Spray the breasts again with oil and continue cooking for 6 to 7 minutes more, until golden and crispy.

PER SERVING: Total calories: 345; Total fat: 18g; Total carbohydrates: 8g; Fiber: 2g; Erythritol: 0g; Net carbs: 6g; Protein: 39g

MACROS: 47% Fat; 45% Protein; 8% Carbs

Buffalo Chicken Wings

PREP TIME: **10 MINUTES** | COOK TIME: **20 TO 25 MINUTES** | TEMPERATURE: **400°F**

If you love chicken wings, you are going to go wild for these. They are crispy perfection, coated in a garlicky sauce with just the right amount of heat. This recipe works just as well for a game-day appetizer as it does for a weeknight meal. **SERVES 4**

KID-FRIENDLY

FAVORITE

2 tablespoons baking powder

1 teaspoon smoked paprika

Sea salt

Freshly ground black pepper

2 pounds chicken wings or chicken drumettes

Avocado oil spray

⅓ cup avocado oil

½ cup Buffalo hot sauce, such as Frank's RedHot

¼ cup (4 tablespoons) unsalted butter

2 tablespoons apple cider vinegar

1 teaspoon minced garlic

Blue Cheese Dressing (page 169) or Garlic Ranch Dressing (page 168), for serving

1. In a large bowl, stir together the baking powder, smoked paprika, and salt and pepper to taste. Add the chicken wings and toss to coat.

2. Set the air fryer to 400°F. Spray the wings with oil.

3. Place the wings in the basket in a single layer, working in batches, and cook for 20 to 25 minutes. Check with an instant-read thermometer and remove when they reach 155°F. Let rest until they reach 165°F.

4. While the wings are cooking, whisk together the avocado oil, hot sauce, butter, vinegar, and garlic in a small saucepan over medium-low heat until warm.

5. When the wings are done cooking, toss them with the Buffalo sauce. Serve warm with the dressing.

PER SERVING: Total calories: 750; Total fat: 64g; Total carbohydrates: 2g; Fiber: <1g; Erythritol: 0g; Net carbs: 2g; Protein: 34g

MACROS: 77% Fat; 18% Protein; 5% Carbs

Broccoli-Stuffed Chicken

PREP TIME: **10 MINUTES** | COOK TIME: **19 TO 24 MINUTES** | TEMPERATURE: **400°F**

When simple and delicious collide, it is a beautiful thing. This recipe is easy to make and is always a hit. I love to watch friends and family gobble it down, always blown away by how ridiculously cheesy and delicious it is. They never suspect that it's part of my keto diet plan. **SERVES 6**

KID-FRIENDLY

1 tablespoon avocado oil

¼ cup chopped onion

½ cup finely chopped broccoli

4 ounces cream cheese, at room temperature

2 ounces Cheddar cheese, shredded

1 teaspoon garlic powder

½ teaspoon sea salt, plus additional for seasoning, divided

¼ freshly ground black pepper, plus additional for seasoning, divided

2 pounds boneless, skinless chicken breasts

1 teaspoon smoked paprika

1. Heat a medium skillet over medium-high heat and pour in the avocado oil. Add the onion and broccoli and cook, stirring occasionally, for 5 to 8 minutes, until the onion is tender.

2. Transfer to a large bowl and stir in the cream cheese, Cheddar cheese, and garlic powder, and season to taste with salt and pepper.

3. Hold a sharp knife parallel to the chicken breast and cut a long pocket into one side. Stuff the chicken pockets with the broccoli mixture, using toothpicks to secure the pockets around the filling.

4. In a small dish, combine the paprika, ½ teaspoon salt, and ¼ teaspoon pepper. Sprinkle this over the outside of the chicken.

5. Set the air fryer to 400°F. Place the chicken in a single layer in the air fryer basket, cooking in batches if necessary, and cook for 14 to 16 minutes, until an instant-read thermometer reads 160°F. Place the chicken on a plate and tent a piece of aluminum foil over the chicken. Allow to rest for 5 to 10 minutes before serving.

Variation tip: If you would like to use boneless chicken thighs instead of breasts, you can. Just pound each thigh thin and place the cheese and broccoli in the center. Starting at the long side, roll the chicken, tucking the edges in as you go. Secure with toothpicks.

PER SERVING: Total calories: 277; Total fat: 15g; Total carbohydrates: 3g; Fiber: 1g; Erythritol: 0g; Net carbs: 2g; Protein: 35g

MACROS: 70% Fat; 24% Protein; 6% Carbs

Chicken Parmesan

PREP TIME: **25 MINUTES** | COOK TIME: **18 TO 20 MINUTES** | TEMPERATURE: **400°F**

For me, few foods are as comforting as juicy, crispy chicken. It is no surprise that this recipe is one of the most requested dinners at my house. Almond flour and Parmesan cheese don't adhere quite as easily as traditional flour and bread crumbs, so use your fingers to gently press the breading into the chicken. For this little bit of extra effort, you will be richly rewarded with perfectly crispy chicken.   SERVES 8

KID-FRIENDLY

FAVORITE

2 pounds boneless, skinless chicken breasts or thighs

1 cup finely ground blanched almond flour

1 cup grated Parmesan cheese

1 teaspoon Italian seasoning

Sea salt

Freshly ground black pepper

2 large eggs

Avocado oil spray

⅓ cup sugar-free marinara sauce

4 ounces fresh mozzarella cheese, sliced or shredded

1. Place the chicken in a zip-top bag or between two pieces of plastic wrap. Use a meat mallet or heavy skillet to pound the chicken to a uniform ½-inch thickness.

2. Place the almond flour, Parmesan cheese, Italian seasoning, and salt and pepper to taste in a large shallow bowl.

3. In a separate shallow bowl, beat the eggs.

4. Dip a chicken breast in the egg, then coat it in the almond flour mixture, making sure to press the coating onto the chicken gently. Repeat with the remaining chicken.

5. Set the air fryer to 400°F. Spray both sides of the chicken well with oil and place the pieces in a single layer in the air fryer basket, working in batches if necessary. Cook for 10 minutes.

6. Flip the chicken with a spatula. Spray each piece with more oil and continue cooking for 5 minutes more.

7. Top each chicken piece with the marinara sauce and mozzarella. Return to the air fryer and cook for 3 to 5 minutes, until the cheese is melted and an instant-read thermometer reads 160°F.

8. Allow the chicken to rest for 5 minutes, then serve.

Cooking tip: If you have time and want to level up the tenderness of your chicken, brine it before you bread it. To do this, heat 1 cup of water over medium heat and stir in ½ cup of salt until the salt dissolves. Transfer to a medium bowl and fill the bowl with cold water. Add the chicken breasts and allow them to brine in the refrigerator for at least 45 minutes. Remove the chicken from the liquid and pat dry. Continue with the recipe as instructed.

PER SERVING: Total calories: 306; Total fat: 17g; Total carbohydrates: 5g; Fiber: 2g; Erythritol: 0g; Net carbs: 3g; Protein: 36g

MACROS: 50% Fat; 47% Protein; 3% Carbs

Lemon-Dijon Boneless Chicken

PREP TIME: **5 MINUTES, PLUS 30 MINUTES TO 4 HOURS TO MARINATE** |
COOK TIME: **13 TO 16 MINUTES** | TEMPERATURE: **400°F**

The secret to incomparably tender chicken breast is a punchy marinade. With tangy Dijon mustard and a kick of heat, this recipe is full of flavor.   SERVES 6

KID-FRIENDLY

½ cup sugar-free mayonnaise (homemade, page 164, or store-bought)

1 tablespoon Dijon mustard

1 tablespoon freshly squeezed lemon juice (optional)

1 tablespoon coconut aminos

1 teaspoon Italian seasoning

1 teaspoon sea salt

½ teaspoon freshly ground black pepper

¼ teaspoon cayenne pepper

1½ pounds boneless, skinless chicken breasts or thighs

1. In a small bowl, combine the mayonnaise, mustard, lemon juice (if using), coconut aminos, Italian seasoning, salt, black pepper, and cayenne pepper.

2. Place the chicken in a shallow dish or large zip-top plastic bag. Add the marinade, making sure all the pieces are coated. Cover and refrigerate for at least 30 minutes or up to 4 hours.

3. Set the air fryer to 400°F. Arrange the chicken in a single layer in the air fryer basket, working in batches if necessary. Cook for 7 minutes. Flip the chicken and continue cooking for 6 to 9 minutes more, until an instant-read thermometer reads 160°F.

Cooking tip: If you plan on marinating the meat for more than 4 hours, I recommend omitting the lemon juice, as it can make the chicken tough if it marinates too long.

PER SERVING: Total calories: 236; Total fat: 17g; Total carbohydrates: 1g; Fiber: <1g; Erythritol: 0g; Net carbs: 1g; Protein: 23g

MACROS: 65% Fat; 35% Protein; 0% Carbs

Spice-Rubbed Turkey Breast

PREP TIME: **5 MINUTES** | COOK TIME: **45 TO 55 MINUTES** | TEMPERATURE: **350°F**

The first time my husband tasted this recipe, he declared that it was just like a dish made in the deep fryer. This crisp, evenly browned, and perfectly roasted turkey is perfect on its own or to use in recipes such as Turkey Pot Pie (page 72).   **SERVES 10**

KID FRIENDLY

1 tablespoon sea salt

1 teaspoon paprika

1 teaspoon onion powder

1 teaspoon garlic powder

½ teaspoon freshly ground black pepper

4 pounds bone-in, skin-on turkey breast

2 tablespoons unsalted butter, melted

1. In a small bowl, combine the salt, paprika, onion powder, garlic powder, and pepper.

2. Sprinkle the seasonings all over the turkey. Brush the turkey with some of the melted butter.

3. Set the air fryer to 350°F. Place the turkey in the air fryer basket, skin-side down, and cook for 25 minutes.

4. Flip the turkey and brush it with the remaining butter. Continue cooking for another 20 to 30 minutes, until an instant-read thermometer reads 160°F.

5. Remove the turkey breast from the air fryer. Tent a piece of aluminum foil over the turkey, and allow it to rest for about 5 minutes before serving.

Air Fryer tip: If you're working with a smaller air fryer than the Philips XXL model, use the largest turkey breast that will fit, and rely on the instant-read thermometer to adjust your cooking time accordingly.

PER SERVING: Total calories: 278; Total fat: 14g; Total carbohydrates: <1g; Fiber: <1g; Erythritol: 0g; Net carbs: <1g; Protein: 34g

MACROS: 45% Fat; 49% Protein; 6% Carbs

Buffalo Chicken Tenders

PREP TIME: **15 MINUTES** | COOK TIME: **7 TO 10 MINUTES** | TEMPERATURE: **400°F**

Buffalo chicken never gets old—as if it isn't obvious by now with the number of Buffalo-style recipes in this cookbook. The casual vibe of this recipe makes it perfect for low-key entertaining. Juicy chicken is fried until crispy and tossed with a classic sauce—both kids and adults go wild for this recipe.   SERVES 4

QUICK

FAVORITE

½ cup finely ground blanched almond flour

½ cup finely grated Parmesan cheese

1 teaspoon smoked paprika

¼ teaspoon cayenne pepper

½ teaspoon sea salt, plus additional for seasoning, divided

Freshly ground black pepper

2 large eggs

1 pound chicken tenders

Avocado oil spray

⅓ cup hot sauce, such as Frank's RedHot

2 tablespoons unsalted butter

2 tablespoons white vinegar

1 garlic clove, minced

Blue Cheese Dressing (page 169), for serving

Blue cheese crumbles, for serving

1. In a shallow bowl, combine the almond flour, Parmesan cheese, smoked paprika, and cayenne pepper and season with salt and pepper to taste. In a separate shallow bowl, beat the eggs.

2. One at a time, dip the chicken tenders in the eggs, then coat them with the almond flour mixture, making sure to press the coating into the chicken gently.

3. Set the air fryer to 400°F. Place the chicken tenders in a single layer in the air fryer basket and spray them with oil. Cook for 4 minutes. Flip the tenders and spray them with more oil. Cook for 3 to 6 minutes more or until an instant-read thermometer reads 165°F.

4. While the chicken is cooking, combine the hot sauce, butter, vinegar, garlic, and ½ teaspoon of salt in a small saucepan over medium-low heat. Heat until the butter is melted, whisking to combine.

5. Toss the chicken tenders with the sauce. Serve warm with Blue Cheese Dressing and blue cheese crumbles.

Cooking tip: Make sure that you only flip the tenders once! Flipping more often causes the breading to fall off.

Variation tip: If Buffalo sauce isn't your thing, you can omit it here and instead coat the tenders in the Barbecue Sauce from the Barbecue Turkey Meatballs, page 68.

PER SERVING: Total calories: 337; Total fat: 20g; Total carbohydrates: 4g; Fiber: 2g; Erythritol: 0g; Net carbs: 2g; Protein: 37g

MACROS: 53% Fat; 44% Protein; 3% Carbs

Nashville Hot Chicken

PREP TIME: **20 MINUTES, PLUS 15 MINUTES TO SET** | COOK TIME: **24 TO 28 MINUTES** |
TEMPERATURE: **400°F, THEN 350°F**

When I was growing up in the South, fried chicken made a regular appearance on our dinner table. This spicy take on the original hot chicken, which originated in Nashville, Tennessee, is a fun twist. To make the chicken even more moist, salt it the day before.   SERVES 8

FAVORITE

3 pounds bone-in, skin-on chicken pieces, breasts halved crosswise

1 tablespoon sea salt

1 tablespoon freshly ground black pepper

1½ cups finely ground blanched almond flour

1½ cups grated Parmesan cheese

1 tablespoon baking powder

2 teaspoons garlic powder, divided

½ cup heavy (whipping) cream

2 large eggs, beaten

1 tablespoon vinegar-based hot sauce

Avocado oil spray

½ cup (1 stick) unsalted butter

½ cup avocado oil

1 tablespoon cayenne pepper (more or less to taste)

2 tablespoons brown sugar substitute, such as Sukrin Gold

1. Sprinkle the chicken with the salt and pepper.

2. In a large shallow bowl, whisk together the almond flour, Parmesan cheese, baking powder, and 1 teaspoon of the garlic powder.

3. In a separate bowl, whisk together the heavy cream, eggs, and hot sauce.

4. Dip the chicken pieces in the egg, then coat each with the almond flour mixture, pressing the mixture into the chicken to adhere. Allow to sit for 15 minutes to let the breading set.

5. Set the air fryer to 400°F. Place the chicken in a single layer in the air fryer basket, being careful not to overcrowd the pieces, working in batches if necessary. Spray the chicken with oil and cook for 13 minutes.

6. Carefully flip the chicken and spray it with more oil. Reduce the air fryer temperature to 350°F. Cook for another 11 to 15 minutes, until an instant-read thermometer reads 160°F.

7. While the chicken cooks, heat the butter, avocado oil, cayenne pepper, brown sugar substitute, and remaining 1 teaspoon of garlic powder in a saucepan over medium-low heat. Cook until the butter is melted and the sugar substitute has dissolved.

8. Remove the chicken from the air fryer. Use tongs to dip the chicken in the sauce. Place the coated chicken on a rack over a baking sheet, and allow it to rest for 5 minutes before serving.

PER SERVING: Total calories: 677; Total fat: 50g; Total carbohydrates: 10g; Fiber: 3g; Erythritol: 3g; Net carbs: 4g; Protein: 52g

MACROS: 66% Fat; 31% Protein; 3% Carbs

Barbecue Turkey Meatballs

PREP TIME: **20 MINUTES** | COOK TIME: **9 TO 12 MINUTES** | TEMPERATURE: **400°F**

We eat a lot of meatballs around our house, and these are a particular favorite. If you think you don't like ground turkey, this is the recipe that will change your mind. Turkey meatballs are so ridiculously tender and flavor-packed, they're sure to be as big a win in your house as they are in mine.   **SERVES 4**

QUICK

KID-FRIENDLY

FAVORITE

1 pound ground turkey

½ teaspoon sea salt, plus additional to season the ground turkey

Freshly ground black pepper

1 large egg, beaten

1 teaspoon gelatin

½ cup almond meal

½ tablespoon chili powder

2½ teaspoons smoked paprika, divided

1 teaspoon onion powder

2 teaspoons garlic powder, divided

Avocado oil spray

¾ cup sugar-free ketchup

1 tablespoon yellow mustard

1 tablespoon apple cider vinegar

2 tablespoons brown sugar substitute, such as Swerve or Sukrin Gold

1 teaspoon liquid smoke

1. Place the ground turkey in a large bowl and season with salt and pepper.

2. Place the beaten egg in a bowl and sprinkle with the gelatin. Allow to sit for 5 minutes, then whisk to combine.

3. Pour the gelatin mixture over the ground turkey and add the almond meal, chili powder, 1 teaspoon of smoked paprika, onion powder, and 1 teaspoon of garlic powder. Mix gently with your hands until combined.

4. Form the mixture into 1½-inch balls.

5. Set the air fryer to 400°F. Spray the meatballs with oil and place in the air fryer basket in a single layer. Cook for 5 minutes. Flip the meatballs and spray them with more oil. Cook for 4 to 7 minutes more, until an instant-read thermometer reads 165°F.

6. While the meatballs cook, place the ketchup, mustard, apple cider vinegar, and brown sugar substitute in a small saucepan over medium heat. Bring to a simmer and cook for 5 minutes. Reduce the heat to low and add the remaining 1½ teaspoons of smoked paprika, liquid smoke, remaining 1 teaspoon of garlic powder, and ½ teaspoon of salt. Cook for 5 minutes more, stirring occasionally, until thickened. Toss the meatballs with the sauce and serve warm.

Cooking tip: I like to use a cookie scoop to form the meatballs. This helps keep them uniform in size, which ensures that they will cook evenly.

PER SERVING: Total calories: 412; Total fat: 24g; Total carbohydrates: 15g; Fiber: 3g; Erythritol: 6g; Net carbs: 6g; Protein: 38g

MACROS: 52% Fat; 37% Protein; 11% Carbs

Chicken Kiev

PREP TIME: 25 MINUTES, PLUS 4 HOURS TO CHILL | **COOK TIME: 14 TO 18 MINUTES** | **TEMPERATURE: 350°F**

Chicken Kiev has always been a favorite around our house. This keto-friendly version is just as delicious as the original, which is considered the pinnacle of Russian cooking. This recipe requires a bit of advance planning, but you will be richly rewarded for your efforts. **SERVES 8**

KID-FRIENDLY

FAVORITE

- ½ cup (1 stick) unsalted butter, at room temperature
- 1 teaspoon minced garlic
- 2 tablespoons chopped fresh parsley
- ½ teaspoon freshly ground black pepper
- 2 pounds boneless, skinless chicken breasts
- Sea salt
- ¾ cup finely ground blanched almond flour
- ¾ cup grated Parmesan cheese
- ⅛ teaspoon cayenne pepper
- 2 large eggs
- Avocado oil spray

1. In a medium bowl, combine the butter, garlic, parsley, and black pepper. Form the mixture into a log and wrap it tightly with parchment paper or plastic wrap. Refrigerate for at least 2 hours, until firm.

2. Place the chicken breasts in a zip-top bag or between two pieces of plastic wrap. Pound the chicken with a meat mallet or heavy skillet to an even ¼-inch thickness.

3. Place a pat of butter in the center of each chicken breast and wrap the chicken tightly around the butter from the long side, tucking in the short sides as you go. Secure with toothpicks. Season the outside of the chicken with salt.

Wrap the stuffed chicken tightly with plastic wrap and refrigerate at least 2 hours or overnight.

4. In a shallow bowl, combine the almond flour, Parmesan cheese, and cayenne pepper.

5. In another shallow bowl, beat the eggs.

6. Dip each piece of chicken in the eggs, then coat it in the almond flour mixture, using your fingers to press the breading gently into the chicken.

7. Set the air fryer to 350°F. Spray the chicken with oil and place it in a single layer in the air fryer basket, working in batches if necessary. Cook for 8 minutes. Flip the chicken, then spray it again with oil. Cook for 6 to 10 minutes more, until an instant-read thermometer reads 165°F.

Cooking tip: If you prefer, you can freeze the butter for 30 minutes to save time.

PER SERVING: Total calories: 333; Total fat: 23g; Total carbohydrates: 3g; Fiber: 1g; Erythritol: 0g; Net carbs: 2g; Protein: 31g

MACROS: 62% Fat; 37% Protein; 1% Carbs

Turkey Pot Pie

PREP TIME: **20 MINUTES** | COOK TIME: **30 TO 35 MINUTES** | TEMPERATURE: **325°F**

Dinner could not be more satisfying and comforting than a rich and creamy pot pie. The whole family is going to love this keto-friendly twist on a classic. Leftovers will keep well in the refrigerator for about 4 days, or they can be frozen for up to 2 months. This is one of my all-time favorites!   SERVES 8

KID-FRIENDLY

FAVORITE

- ¼ cup (4 tablespoons) unsalted butter
- 2 shallots, minced
- 1 cup mushrooms, chopped
- 2 celery stalks, chopped
- 1 teaspoon minced garlic
- 1 teaspoon sea salt
- ¼ teaspoon freshly ground black pepper
- 1¾ cups turkey broth or chicken broth
- ⅔ cup heavy (whipping) cream
- 2 ounces cream cheese
- ½ teaspoon xanthan gum
- 3 cups chopped cooked turkey
- ½ cup frozen baby peas (optional)
- 1 recipe Fathead Pizza Dough (page 171)

1. Melt the butter in a large saucepan over medium heat. Add the shallots, mushrooms, and celery. Cook for 5 minutes, stirring frequently. Add the garlic, salt, and pepper and cook for 1 minute more.

2. Stir in the broth, heavy cream, cream cheese, and xanthan gum. Bring to a simmer and cook for 1 minute, stirring constantly. Reduce the heat to low and cook for 5 minutes, stirring often, until thickened.

3. Stir in the turkey and peas (if using).

4. Divide the mixture among 8 individual ramekins.

5. Roll out the pizza dough between two sheets of parchment paper. Cut the dough into pieces large enough to cover each ramekin, and place them over the filling. Using a sharp knife, cut a slit or two in the top of each crust to vent.

6. Set the air fryer to 325°F. Place the ramekins in the air fryer basket and cook for 18 to 23 minutes, until the crusts are golden brown.

Ingredient tip: While some people don't consider baby peas to be keto-friendly, many people enjoy them in small quantities. If they work with your macros and you enjoy them, they are fabulous here.

PER SERVING: Total calories: 359; Total fat: 32g; Total carbohydrates: 7g; Fiber: 2g; Erythritol: 0g; Net carbs: 5g; Protein: 17g

MACROS: 80% Fat; 19% Protein; 1% Carbs

Smoky Chicken Leg Quarters

PREP TIME: **5 MINUTES, PLUS 2 HOURS TO MARINATE** | COOK TIME: **23 TO 27 MINUTES** | TEMPERATURE: **400°F, THEN 350°F**

This recipe was born a few years back when I was trying to blend my boys' infinite ability to make chicken legs disappear with my need for tasty meals that don't break my budget. Originally, I baked these, but they are even better in the air fryer. I often double this recipe—leftovers are great pulled from the bone and added to salads or baked in casseroles. **SERVES 6**

KID FRIENDLY

½ cup avocado oil

2 teaspoons smoked paprika

1 teaspoon sea salt

1 teaspoon garlic powder

½ teaspoon dried rosemary

½ teaspoon dried thyme

½ teaspoon freshly ground black pepper

2 pounds bone-in, skin-on chicken leg quarters

1. In a blender or small bowl, combine the avocado oil, smoked paprika, salt, garlic powder, rosemary, thyme, and black pepper.

2. Place the chicken in a shallow dish or large zip-top bag. Pour the marinade over the chicken, making sure all the legs are coated. Cover and marinate for at least 2 hours or overnight.

3. Place the chicken in a single layer in the air fryer basket, working in batches if necessary. Set the air fryer to 400°F and cook for 15 minutes. Flip the chicken legs, then reduce the temperature to 350°F. Cook for 8 to 12 minutes more, until an instant-read thermometer reads 160°F when inserted into the thickest piece of chicken.

4. Allow to rest for 5 to 10 minutes before serving.

PER SERVING: Total calories: 569; Total fat: 53g; Total carbohydrates: 1g; Fiber: <1g; Erythritol: 0g; Net carbs: 1g; Protein: 23g

MACROS: 84% Fat; 16% Protein; 0% Carbs

Chicken Paillard

PREP TIME: **20 MINUTES** | COOK TIME: **7 TO 10 MINUTES** | TEMPERATURE: **400°F**

When you need to relieve a little stress, Chicken Paillard is the dinner for you. Pounding the meat until it is thin allows it to cook quickly and retain a wildly delicious flavor. I like to serve this over a mixed green salad with warm feta cheese for a simple meal that never fails to satisfy. Stress relief and a delicious meal, all in one! **SERVES 4**

QUICK

KID-FRIENDLY

5-INGREDIENT

1 pound boneless, skinless chicken breasts or thighs

2 tablespoons avocado oil

1 tablespoon freshly squeezed lemon juice

1 teaspoon chopped fresh oregano

½ teaspoon garlic powder

Sea salt

Freshly ground black pepper

1. Place the chicken in a zip-top bag or between two pieces of plastic wrap. Using a meat mallet or a heavy skillet, pound the chicken until it is very thin, about ¼ inch thick.

2. In a small bowl, combine the avocado oil, lemon juice, oregano, garlic powder, salt, and pepper. Place the chicken in a shallow dish and pour the marinade over it. Toss to coat all the chicken, and let it rest at room temperature for 10 to 15 minutes.

3. Set the air fryer to 400°F. Place the chicken in a single layer in the air fryer basket and cook for 5 minutes. Flip and cook for another 2 to 5 minutes, until an instant-read thermometer reads 160°F. Allow to rest for 5 minutes before serving.

Cooking tip: For especially thick chicken breasts, you may want to butterfly them before pounding. To do this, hold a knife parallel to the chicken and slice through it, stopping short of the other side. Open the chicken (like a book), and then pound it thin.

PER SERVING: Total calories: 178; Total fat: 10g; Total carbohydrates: 1g; Fiber: <1g; Erythritol: 0g; Net carbs: 1g; Protein: 23g

MACROS: 51% Fat; 49% Protein; 0% Carbs

Tex-Mex Chicken Roll-Ups

PREP TIME: **10 MINUTES** | COOK TIME: **14 TO 17 MINUTES** | TEMPERATURE: **350°F**

Chicken roll-ups aren't as labor-intensive as they sound, and they are always a crowd-pleaser. I like to make these ahead of time so all I have to do is pull them from the fridge and pop them in the air fryer. Serve with cauliflower rice mixed with chopped cilantro and lime juice.   **SERVES 8**

QUICK

2 pounds boneless, skinless chicken breasts or thighs

1 teaspoon chili powder

½ teaspoon smoked paprika

½ teaspoon ground cumin

Sea salt

Freshly ground black pepper

6 ounces Monterey Jack cheese, shredded

4 ounces canned diced green chiles

Avocado oil spray

1. Place the chicken in a large zip-top bag or between two pieces of plastic wrap. Using a meat mallet or heavy skillet, pound the chicken until it is about ¼ inch thick.

2. In a small bowl, combine the chili powder, smoked paprika, cumin, and salt and pepper to taste. Sprinkle both sides of the chicken with the seasonings.

3. Sprinkle the chicken with the Monterey Jack cheese, then the diced green chiles.

4. Roll up each piece of chicken from the long side, tucking in the ends as you go. Secure the roll-up with a toothpick.

5. Set the air fryer to 350°F. Spray the outside of the chicken with avocado oil. Place the chicken in a single layer in the basket, working in batches if necessary, and cook for 7 minutes. Flip and cook for another 7 to 10 minutes, until an instant-read thermometer reads 160°F.

6. Remove the chicken from the air fryer and allow it to rest for about 5 minutes before serving.

PER SERVING: Total calories: 192; Total fat: 9g; Total carbohydrates: 1g; Fiber: 1g; Erythritol: 0g; Net carbs: 0g; Protein: 28g

MACROS: 42% Fat; 58% Protein; 0% Carbs

Jalapeño Popper Chicken

PREP TIME: **10 MINUTES** | COOK TIME: **14 TO 17 MINUTES** | TEMPERATURE: **350°F**

I never get tired of Jalapeño Poppers (page 42), and this recipe provides an extra dose of the flavors I love. I recommend wearing disposable kitchen gloves when seeding and dicing the jalapeños so you don't accidentally touch (and burn!) your eyes later in the day. **SERVES 8**

QUICK

FAVORITE

5-INGREDIENT

2 pounds boneless, skinless chicken breasts or thighs

Sea salt

Freshly ground black pepper

8 ounces cream cheese, at room temperature

4 ounces Cheddar cheese, shredded

2 jalapeños, seeded and diced

1 teaspoon minced garlic

Avocado oil spray

1. Place the chicken in a large zip-top bag or between two pieces of plastic wrap. Using a meat mallet or heavy skillet, pound the chicken until it is about ¼-inch thick. Season both sides of the chicken with salt and pepper.

2. In a medium bowl, combine the cream cheese, Cheddar cheese, jalapeños, and garlic. Divide the mixture among the chicken pieces. Roll up each piece from the long side, tucking in the ends as you go. Secure with toothpicks.

3. Set the air fryer to 350°F. Spray the outside of the chicken with oil. Place the chicken in a single layer in the air fryer basket, working in batches if necessary, and cook for 7 minutes. Flip the chicken and cook for another 7 to 10 minutes, until an instant-read thermometer reads 160°F.

Substitution tip: Feel free to change up the cheeses here. Mascarpone is nice instead of cream cheese, and feta or Monterey Jack are great alternatives to Cheddar.

PER SERVING: Total calories: 264; Total fat: 17g; Total carbohydrates: 2g; Fiber: <1g; Erythritol: 0g; Net carbs: 2g; Protein: 28g

MACROS: 58% Fat; 42% Protein; 0% Carbs

Coconut Shrimp, page 88

5

Seafood

Maple-Glazed Salmon with a Kick

PREP TIME: **5 MINUTES** | COOK TIME: **23 MINUTES** | TEMPERATURE: **300°F, THEN 400°F**

My husband's favorite fish is salmon, and I came up with this dish when he asked for something different. He loves the sweet glaze that has just the right amount of kick. **SERVES 4**

QUICK

½ cup maple syrup substitute, such as ChocZero sugar-free maple syrup

1 tablespoon grated fresh ginger

2 tablespoons coconut aminos

2 tablespoons freshly squeezed lemon juice

1 teaspoon minced garlic

Sea salt

Freshly ground black pepper

1 pound (1½-inch-thick) salmon fillets

Avocado oil spray

1. In a small dish that fits inside your air fryer, combine the maple syrup substitute with the ginger, coconut aminos, lemon juice, and garlic. Season with salt and pepper.

2. Set the air fryer to 300°F. Place the dish in the basket and cook for 15 minutes, stirring every 5 minutes.

3. Divide the glaze between 2 bowls and allow it to cool slightly. Brush the salmon with the glaze from one bowl, and spray both sides of the fillets with oil. Place the fillets in a single layer in the air fryer basket, skin-side up.

4. Set the air fryer to 400°F and cook for 7 minutes. Flip and cook for 1 minute longer or until an instant-read thermometer reads about 125°F for medium-rare.

5. Let rest for 5 minutes, then serve with the reserved sauce from the second bowl.

PER SERVING: Total calories: 215; Total fat: 4g; Total carbohydrates: 33g; Fiber: 28g; Erythritol: 0g; Net carbs: 5g; Protein: 23g

MACROS: 17% Fat; 43% Protein; 40% Carbs

Fish Fillets with Lemon-Dill Sauce

PREP TIME: **5 MINUTES** | COOK TIME: **7 MINUTES** | TEMPERATURE: **400°F, THEN 325°F**

Don't you love no-fuss meals? This simple recipe is tasty enough to serve for company but easy enough for a busy weeknight. I call it winning anytime you can get dinner on the table in less than 15 minutes. **SERVES 4**

QUICK

5-INGREDIENT

1 pound snapper, grouper, or salmon fillets

Sea salt

Freshly ground black pepper

1 tablespoon avocado oil

¼ cup sour cream

¼ cup sugar-free mayonnaise (homemade, page 164, or store-bought)

2 tablespoons fresh dill, chopped, plus more for garnish

1 tablespoon freshly squeezed lemon juice

½ teaspoon grated lemon zest

1. Pat the fish dry with paper towels and season well with salt and pepper. Brush with the avocado oil.

2. Set the air fryer to 400°F. Place the fillets in the air fryer basket and cook for 1 minute.

3. Lower the air fryer temperature to 325°F and continue cooking for 5 minutes. Flip the fish and cook for 1 minute more or until an instant-read thermometer reads 145°F. (If using salmon, cook it to 125°F for medium-rare.)

4. While the fish is cooking, make the sauce by combining the sour cream, mayonnaise, dill, lemon juice, and lemon zest in a medium bowl. Season with salt and pepper and stir until combined. Refrigerate until ready to serve.

5. Serve the fish with the sauce, garnished with the remaining dill.

PER SERVING: Total calories: 304; Total fat: 19g; Total carbohydrates: 2g; Fiber: 0g; Erythritol: 0g; Net carbs: 2g; Protein: 30g

MACROS: 56% Fat; 39% Protein; 5% Carbs

Shrimp Caesar Salad

PREP TIME: **10 MINUTES, PLUS 15 MINUTES TO MARINATE** | COOK TIME: **4 TO 6 MINUTES** | TEMPERATURE: **400°F**

When the weather gets warm, I love salad for dinner. This supper salad is a particular favorite of mine. The simple shrimp marinade and delicious home-made dressing play together to keep the flavors perky and bright. If you are pressed for time, however, feel free to use a store-bought Caesar dressing; most store-bought versions are keto-friendly, but, as always, check the label. I am a big fan of the Primal Kitchen brand, thanks to their clean ingredients and great flavors. **SERVES 4**

QUICK

FAVORITE

12 ounces fresh large shrimp, peeled and deveined

1 tablespoon plus 1 teaspoon freshly squeezed lemon juice, divided

4 tablespoons olive oil or avocado oil, divided

2 garlic cloves, minced, divided

¼ teaspoon sea salt, plus additional to season the marinade

¼ teaspoon freshly ground black pepper, plus additional to season the marinade

⅓ cup sugar-free mayonnaise (homemade, page 164, or store-bought)

2 tablespoons freshly grated Parmesan cheese

1 teaspoon Dijon mustard

1 tinned anchovy, mashed

12 ounces romaine hearts, torn

1. Place the shrimp in a large bowl. Add 1 tablespoon of lemon juice, 1 tablespoon of olive oil, and 1 minced garlic clove. Season with salt and pepper. Toss well and refrigerate for 15 minutes.

2. While the shrimp marinates, make the dressing: In a blender, combine the mayonnaise, Parmesan cheese, Dijon mustard, the remaining 1 teaspoon of lemon juice, the anchovy, the remaining minced garlic clove, ¼ teaspoon of salt, and ¼ teaspoon of pepper. Process until smooth. With the blender running, slowly stream in the remaining

3 tablespoons of oil. Transfer the mixture to a jar; seal and refrigerate until ready to serve.

3. Remove the shrimp from its marinade and place it in the air fryer basket in a single layer. Set the air fryer to 400°F and cook for 2 minutes. Flip the shrimp and cook for 2 to 4 minutes more, until the flesh turns opaque.

4. Place the romaine in a large bowl and toss with the desired amount of dressing. Top with the shrimp and serve immediately.

Variation tip: If you like heat—and I do—add ¼ teaspoon of red pepper flakes or ⅛ teaspoon of cayenne pepper to the marinade.

PER SERVING: Total calories: 329; Total fat: 30g; Total carbohydrates: 4g; Fiber: 2g; Erythritol: 0g; Net carbs: 2g; Protein: 16g

MACROS: 82% Fat; 18% Protein; 0% Carbs

Crab Cakes

PREP TIME: **10 MINUTES, PLUS 1 HOUR TO CHILL** | COOK TIME: **14 MINUTES** |
TEMPERATURE: **400°F**

Crab cakes always feel like a treat, but these are all the more enjoyable because they are easy to make. The air fryer shines here, delivering perfectly cooked patties that don't fall apart. I like to serve these on a bed of arugula, or with Lemon-Thyme Asparagus (page 48) on the side. Don't forget the tartar sauce! **SERVES 4**

FAVORITE

Avocado oil spray

⅓ cup red onion, diced

¼ cup red bell pepper, diced

8 ounces lump crabmeat, picked over for shells

3 tablespoons finely ground blanched almond flour

1 large egg, beaten

1 tablespoon sugar-free mayonnaise (homemade, page 164, or store-bought)

2 teaspoons Dijon mustard

⅛ teaspoon cayenne pepper

Sea salt

Freshly ground black pepper

Elevated Tartar Sauce (page 163), for serving

Lemon wedges, for serving

1. Spray an air fryer–friendly baking pan with oil. Put the onion and red bell pepper in the pan and give them a quick spray with oil. Place the pan in the air fryer basket. Set the air fryer to 400°F and cook the vegetables for 7 minutes, until tender.

2. Transfer the vegetables to a large bowl. Add the crabmeat, almond flour, egg, mayonnaise, mustard, and cayenne pepper and season with salt and pepper. Stir until the mixture is well combined.

3. Form the mixture into four 1-inch-thick cakes. Cover with plastic wrap and refrigerate for 1 hour.

4. Place the crab cakes in a single layer in the air fryer basket and spray them with oil.

5. Cook for 4 minutes. Flip the crab cakes and spray with more oil. Cook for 3 minutes more, until the internal temperature of the crab cakes reaches 155°F.

6. Serve with tartar sauce and a squeeze of fresh lemon juice.

Variation tip: If you have it on hand, a teaspoon of Old Bay seasoning is a great addition to the crab cake mixture.

PER SERVING: Total calories: 121; Total fat: 8g; Total carbohydrates: 3g; Fiber: 1g; Erythritol: 0g; Net carbs: 2g; Protein: 11g

MACROS: 60% Fat; 36% Protein; 4% Carbs

Scallops with Lemon-Butter Sauce

PREP TIME: **5 MINUTES, PLUS 15 MINUTES TO CHILL** | COOK TIME: **15 MINUTES** | TEMPERATURE: **350°F**

Plump, meaty scallops drenched in a lemon-butter sauce is a tasty combination suitable for a fancy restaurant. Serve this with crispy Roasted Brussels Sprouts with Bacon (page 41), and get ready to receive rave reviews. SERVES 4

5-INGREDIENT

1 pound large sea scallops

Sea salt

Freshly ground black pepper

Avocado oil spray

¼ cup (4 tablespoons) unsalted butter

1 tablespoon freshly squeezed lemon juice

1 teaspoon minced garlic

¼ teaspoon red pepper flakes

1. If your scallops still have the adductor muscles attached, remove them. Pat the scallops dry with a paper towel.

2. Season the scallops with salt and pepper, then place them on a plate and refrigerate for 15 minutes.

3. Spray the air fryer basket with oil, and arrange the scallops in a single layer. Spray the top of the scallops with oil.

4. Set the air fryer to 350°F and cook for 6 minutes. Flip the scallops and cook for 6 minutes more, until an instant-read thermometer reads 145°F.

5. While the scallops cook, place the butter, lemon juice, garlic, and red pepper flakes in a small ramekin.

6. When the scallops have finished cooking, remove them from the air fryer. Place the ramekin in the air fryer and cook until the butter melts, about 3 minutes. Stir.

7. Toss the scallops with the warm butter and serve.

PER SERVING: Total calories: 203; Total fat: 12g; Total carbohydrates: 3g; Fiber: 0g; Erythritol: 0g; Net carbs: 3g; Protein: 19g

MACROS: 53% Fat; 37% Protein; 10% Carbs

Marinated Swordfish Skewers

PREP TIME: **10 MINUTES, PLUS 30 MINUTES TO MARINATE** | COOK TIME: **6 TO 8 MINUTES** | TEMPERATURE: **400°F**

I have a set of skewers and a holder made for the air fryer, but any skewers that fit in your machine will work. If you use wooden skewers, make sure you soak them in water for the 30 minutes that the fish is marinating. Otherwise, they can be a fire risk. **SERVES 4**

5-INGREDIENT

1 pound filleted swordfish

¼ cup avocado oil

2 tablespoons freshly squeezed lemon juice

1 tablespoon minced fresh parsley

2 teaspoons Dijon mustard

Sea salt

Freshly ground black pepper

3 ounces cherry tomatoes

1. Cut the fish into 1½-inch chunks, picking out any remaining bones.

2. In a large bowl, whisk together the oil, lemon juice, parsley, and Dijon mustard. Season to taste with salt and pepper. Add the fish and toss to coat the pieces. Cover and marinate the fish chunks in the refrigerator for 30 minutes.

3. Remove the fish from the marinade. Thread the fish and cherry tomatoes on 4 skewers, alternating as you go.

4. Set the air fryer to 400°F. Place the skewers in the air fryer basket and cook for 3 minutes. Flip the skewers and cook for 3 to 5 minutes longer, until the fish is cooked through and an instant-read thermometer reads 140°F.

PER SERVING: Total calories: 315; Total fat: 20g; Total carbohydrates: 2g; Fiber: <1g; Erythritol: 0g; Net carbs: 2g; Protein: 29g

MACROS: 57% Fat; 37% Protein; 6% Carbs

Coconut Shrimp

PREP TIME: **15 MINUTES** | COOK TIME: **17 MINUTES** | TEMPERATURE: **400°F**

Coconut shrimp always takes me back to my first cruise in my early twenties. I remember munching on them while looking out over the ocean, thinking that life couldn't get much better. This simple recipe transports me back to that place, and I think you will agree that it deserves a spot in your weekly meal rotation. Serve these with Sriracha Mayonnaise (page 165). **SERVES 4**

FAVORITE

KID-FRIENDLY

¾ cup unsweetened shredded coconut

¾ cup coconut flour

1 teaspoon garlic powder

¼ teaspoon cayenne pepper

Sea salt

Freshly ground black pepper

2 large eggs

1 pound fresh extra-large or jumbo shrimp, peeled and deveined

Avocado oil spray

1. In a medium bowl, combine the shredded coconut, coconut flour, garlic powder, and cayenne pepper. Season to taste with salt and pepper.

2. In a small bowl, beat the eggs.

3. Pat the shrimp dry with paper towels. Dip each shrimp in the eggs and then the coconut mixture. Gently press the coating to the shrimp to help it adhere.

4. Set the air fryer to 400°F. Spray the shrimp with oil and place them in a single layer in the air fryer basket, working in batches if necessary.

5. Cook the shrimp for 9 minutes, then flip and spray them with more oil. Cook for 8 minutes more, until the center of the shrimp is opaque and cooked through.

PER SERVING: Total calories: 362; Total fat: 17g; Total carbohydrates: 20g; Fiber: 11g; Erythritol: 0g; Net carbs: 9g; Protein: 35g

MACROS: 42% Fat; 39% Protein; 19% Carbs

Crispy Fish Sticks

PREP TIME: **10 MINUTES, PLUS 30 MINUTES TO FREEZE** | COOK TIME: **9 MINUTES** | TEMPERATURE: **400°F**

It is a universal law that all kids love fish sticks, and this version is every bit as enticing as the ones you ate growing up (with a lot fewer carbs!). I like to serve them with tartar sauce and a quick slaw salad for a complete meal.   SERVES 4

FAVORITE

KID-FRIENDLY

1 pound cod fillets

1½ cups finely ground blanched almond flour

2 teaspoons Old Bay seasoning

½ teaspoon paprika

Sea salt

Freshly ground black pepper

¼ cup sugar-free mayonnaise (homemade, page 164, or store-bought)

1 large egg, beaten

Avocado oil spray

Elevated Tartar Sauce (page 163), for serving

1. Cut the fish into ¾-inch-wide strips.

2. In a shallow bowl, stir together the almond flour, Old Bay seasoning, paprika, and salt and pepper to taste. In another shallow bowl, whisk together the mayonnaise and egg.

3. Dip the cod strips in the egg mixture, then the almond flour, gently pressing with your fingers to help adhere the coating.

4. Place the coated fish on a parchment paper–lined baking sheet and freeze for 30 minutes.

5. Spray the air fryer basket with oil. Set the air fryer to 400°F. Place the fish in the basket in a single layer, and spray each piece with oil.

6. Cook for 5 minutes. Flip and spray with more oil. Cook for 4 minutes more, until the internal temperature reaches 140°F. Serve with the tartar sauce.

PER SERVING: Total calories: 439; Total fat: 33g; Total carbohydrates: 9g; Fiber: 5g; Erythritol: 0g; Net carbs: 4g; Protein: 31g

MACROS: 68% Fat; 28% Protein; 4% Carbs

Sweet and Spicy Salmon

PREP TIME: **5 MINUTES** | COOK TIME: **10 TO 12 MINUTES** | TEMPERATURE: **400°F**

This is a super-quick main course that you will turn to again and again. It is what I make when I am craving serious flavors and don't have much time. Feel free to experiment with the heat level from the chipotle chile, adding more or less to suit your palate. Whatever you do, don't skip processing the sauce in the blender or food processor, which prevents it from becoming grainy. **SERVES 4**

QUICK

5-INGREDIENT

½ cup sugar-free mayonnaise (homemade, page 164, or store-bought)

2 tablespoons brown sugar substitute, such as Sukrin Gold

2 teaspoons Dijon mustard

1 canned chipotle chile in adobo sauce, diced

1 teaspoon adobo sauce (from the canned chipotle)

16 ounces salmon fillets

Salt

Freshly ground black pepper

1. In a small food processor, combine the mayonnaise, brown sugar substitute, Dijon mustard, chipotle pepper, and adobo sauce. Process for 1 minute until everything is combined and the brown sugar substitute is no longer granular.

2. Season the salmon with salt and pepper. Spread half of the sauce over the fish, and reserve the remainder of the sauce for serving.

3. Set the air fryer to 400°F. Place the salmon in the air fryer basket. Cook for 5 minutes. Flip the salmon and cook for 5 to 7 minutes more, until an instant-read thermometer reads 125°F (for medium-rare).

4. Serve warm with the remaining sauce.

PER SERVING: Total calories: 326; Total fat: 25g; Total carbohydrates: 7g; Fiber: 0g; Erythritol: 6g; Net carbs: 1g; Protein: 23g

MACROS: 69% Fat; 28% Protein; 3% Carbs

Garlic Shrimp

PREP TIME: **5 MINUTES** | COOK TIME: **8 TO 10 MINUTES** | TEMPERATURE: **350°F**

I have always had a soft spot for shrimp, and garlic shrimp is one of my favorite meals. I try to keep raw, cleaned shrimp in my freezer at all times, because they thaw out so quickly—it's a great way to have dinner on the table in less than 20 minutes. **SERVES 4**

QUICK

5-INGREDIENT

1 pound fresh large shrimp, peeled and deveined

1 tablespoon avocado oil

2 teaspoons minced garlic, divided

½ teaspoon red pepper flakes

Sea salt

Freshly ground black pepper

2 tablespoons unsalted butter, melted

2 tablespoons chopped fresh parsley

1. Place the shrimp in a large bowl and toss with the avocado oil, 1 teaspoon of minced garlic, and red pepper flakes. Season with salt and pepper.

2. Set the air fryer to 350°F. Arrange the shrimp in a single layer in the air fryer basket, working in batches if necessary. Cook for 6 minutes. Flip the shrimp and cook for 2 to 4 minutes more, until the internal temperature of the shrimp reaches 120°F. (The time it takes to cook will depend on the size of the shrimp.)

3. While the shrimp are cooking, melt the butter in a small saucepan over medium heat and stir in the remaining 1 teaspoon of garlic.

4. Transfer the cooked shrimp to a large bowl, add the garlic butter, and toss well. Top with the parsley and serve warm.

Ingredient tip: I use avocado oil here because the smoke point for extra-virgin olive oil is 320°F. If you have olive oil that isn't extra-virgin, feel free to use it instead.

PER SERVING: Total calories: 220; Total fat: 11g; Total carbohydrates: 1g; Fiber: <1g; Erythritol: 0g; Net carbs: 1g; Protein: 28g

MACROS: 45% Fat; 51% Protein; 4% Carbs

Tenderloin with Crispy Shallots, page 115

6

Beef

Garlic-Marinated Flank Steak

PREP TIME: **5 MINUTES, PLUS 2 HOURS TO MARINATE** | COOK TIME: **8 TO 10 MINUTES**
(FOR MEDIUM-RARE) | TEMPERATURE: **400°F**

The men in our family have always been snobs when it comes to beef, prefer-ring tenderloin and rib eyes to more economical cuts. As the boys have grown (along with their appetites), the need to change their mind became very real for the sake of our budget. This is the recipe that did it! SERVES 6

KID-FRIENDLY

FAVORITE

½ cup avocado oil

¼ cup coconut aminos

1 shallot, minced

1 tablespoon minced garlic

2 tablespoons chopped fresh oregano, or 2 teaspoons dried

1½ teaspoons sea salt

1 teaspoon freshly ground black pepper

¼ teaspoon red pepper flakes

2 pounds flank steak

1. In a blender, combine the avocado oil, coconut aminos, shallot, garlic, oregano, salt, black pepper, and red pepper flakes. Process until smooth.

2. Place the steak in a zip-top plastic bag or shallow dish with the marinade. Seal the bag or cover the dish and marinate in the refrigerator for at least 2 hours or overnight.

3. Remove the steak from the bag and discard the marinade.

4. Set the air fryer to 400°F. Place the steak in the air fryer basket (if needed, cut into sections and work in batches). Cook for 4 to 6 minutes, flip the steak, and cook for another 4 minutes or until the internal temperature reaches 120°F in the thickest part for medium-rare (or as desired).

PER SERVING: Total calories: 304; Total fat: 23g; Total carbohydrates: 4g; Fiber: <1g; Erythritol: 0g; Net carbs: 4g; Protein: 16g

MACROS: 68% Fat; 21% Protein; 11% Carbs

Greek Beef Kebabs with Tzatziki

PREP TIME: **15 MINUTES, PLUS 4 HOURS TO MARINATE** | COOK TIME: **8 TO 10 MINUTES** | TEMPERATURE: **400°F**

I've always thought of kebabs as summer fare, because they can be quickly and easily cooked on the grill. It turns out, the air fryer makes them something you can enjoy year-round. Serve these with tzatziki sauce. **SERVES 6**

KID-FRIENDLY

1 pound boneless sirloin steak, cut into 2-inch chunks

¼ cup avocado oil

2 teaspoons minced garlic

2 teaspoons dried oregano

Sea salt

Freshly ground black pepper

1 small red onion, cut into wedges

½ cup cherry tomatoes

Tzatziki Sauce (page 170)

4 ounces feta cheese, crumbled

1. Place the steak in a shallow dish.

2. In a blender, combine the avocado oil, garlic, oregano, and salt and pepper to taste. Blend until smooth, then pour over the steak. Cover the dish with plastic wrap and allow to marinate in the refrigerator for at least 4 hours or overnight.

3. Thread the steak, onion, and cherry tomatoes onto 6 skewers, alternating as you go. (If using wooden skewers, first soak them in water for 30 minutes.)

4. Set the air fryer to 400°F. Place the skewers in the basket and cook for 5 minutes. Flip and cook for 3 to 5 minutes more.

5. Transfer the kebabs to serving plates. Drizzle with Tzatziki Sauce and sprinkle with the crumbled feta cheese.

PER SERVING: Total calories: 307; Total fat: 25g; Total carbohydrates: 3g; Fiber: 1g; Erythritol: 0g; Net carbs: 2g; Protein: 18g

MACROS: 73% Fat; 23% Protein; 4% Carbs

Bacon Cheeseburger Meatloaf

PREP TIME: **20 MINUTES** │ COOK TIME: **40 TO 43 MINUTES** │ TEMPERATURE: **400°F**

One of the biggest challenges about the keto diet can be finding meals that the whole family will love. This recipe checks all the boxes, pleasing kids and adults alike. I like to serve it with Lemon-Thyme Asparagus (page 48) or a simple garden salad to balance out the richness.   SERVES 6

KID-FRIENDLY

¼ cup beef broth

2 tablespoons heavy (whipping) cream

2½ teaspoons unflavored gelatin

Avocado oil spray

¼ cup chopped onion

4 ounces (½ cup) keto-friendly tomato sauce

⅓ cup sugar-free mayonnaise (homemade, page 164, or store-bought)

2 tablespoons keto-friendly ketchup

1 large egg, beaten

1 pound ground beef

Sea salt

Freshly ground black pepper

4 slices Cheddar cheese

8 ounces sliced bacon, cooked and crumbled

1 small tomato, sliced

1. Combine the broth and heavy cream in a small bowl. Sprinkle the gelatin evenly over the top. Set aside.

2. Spray a small skillet with oil and place it over medium-high heat. Once the oil is hot, add the onion and cook for 5 minutes or until soft.

3. Reduce the heat to medium-low, then stir the gelatin mixture and add it to the skillet, along with the tomato sauce. Cook, stirring occasionally, until the mixture is reduced by half, about 10 minutes.

4. Meanwhile, stir together the mayonnaise and ketchup in a small bowl.

5. In a large bowl, combine the onion mixture with the egg and ground beef. Season with salt and pepper. Mix well to combine.

6. Place the meatloaf mixture in a small loaf pan that fits inside your air fryer. (I use a 7-by-4-inch pan.) Place the pan in the air fryer basket.

7. Set the air fryer to 400°F and cook for 20 minutes.

8. Top the meatloaf with the mayonnaise sauce, cheese, crumbled bacon, and tomato slices.

9. Cook for 5 to 8 minutes more, until the cheese is melted and an instant-read thermometer reads 160°F.

Substitution tip: The gelatin helps the meatloaf hold its structure in the absence of bread crumbs. If you don't have it on hand, feel free to leave it out of the recipe. If you like, you can use 2 tablespoons of finely ground flaxseeds in place of the gelatin.

PER SERVING: Total calories: 489; Total fat: 41g; Total carbohydrates: 3g; Fiber: 1g; Erythritol: 0g; Net carbs: 2g; Protein: 25g

MACROS: 75% Fat; 20% Protein; 5% Carbs

Spaghetti Zoodles and Meatballs

PREP TIME: **15 MINUTES, PLUS 1 HOUR TO CHILL** | COOK TIME: **11 TO 13 MINUTES** | TEMPERATURE: **400°F**

In my book, comfort food doesn't get any better than spaghetti and meatballs. This low-carb version has all the flavor and none of the carbs. Even picky kids will approve. SERVES 6

KID-FRIENDLY

1 pound ground beef

1½ teaspoons sea salt, plus more for seasoning

1 large egg, beaten

1 teaspoon gelatin

¾ cup Parmesan cheese

2 teaspoons minced garlic

1 teaspoon Italian seasoning

Freshly ground black pepper

Avocado oil spray

Keto-friendly marinara sauce, such as Rao's Homemade®, for serving

6 ounces zucchini noodles, made using a spiralizer or store-bought

1. Place the ground beef in a large bowl, and season with the salt.

2. Place the egg in a separate bowl and sprinkle with the gelatin. Allow to sit for 5 minutes.

3. Stir the gelatin mixture, then pour it over the ground beef. Add the Parmesan, garlic, and Italian seasoning. Season with salt and pepper.

4. Form the mixture into 1½-inch meatballs and place them on a plate; cover with plastic wrap and refrigerate for at least 1 hour or overnight.

5. Spray the meatballs with oil. Set the air fryer to 400°F and arrange the meatballs in a single layer in the air fryer basket. Cook for 4 minutes. Flip the meatballs and spray them with more oil. Cook for 4 minutes more, until an instant-read thermometer reads 160°F. Transfer the meatballs to a plate and allow them to rest.

6. While the meatballs are resting, heat the marinara in a saucepan on the stove over medium heat.

7. Place the zucchini noodles in the air fryer, and cook at 400°F for 3 to 5 minutes.

8. To serve, place the zucchini noodles in serving bowls. Top with meatballs and warm marinara.

Substitution tip: I like to use gelatin because it helps the structure of the meatballs. If you don't have it on hand, you can help bind the meatballs with 2 tablespoons of very finely ground flaxseeds. Or skip both! I've made it all three ways, and they all work.

PER SERVING: Total calories: 312; Total fat: 25g; Total carbohydrates: 2g; Fiber: 1g; Erythritol: 0g; Net carbs: 1g; Protein: 20g

MACROS: 72% Fat; 26% Protein; 2% Carbs

Short Ribs with Chimichurri

PREP TIME: **15 MINUTES, PLUS 45 MINUTES TO REST** | COOK TIME: **13 MINUTES** | TEMPERATURE: **400°F**

The first time I tasted boneless short ribs paired with this chimichurri sauce, I squealed with delight. I like to make a double batch of the sauce. In addition to being wonderful over steak, it is also a great way to brighten up vegetables and chicken. **SERVES 4**

KID-FRIENDLY

FAVORITE

- 1 pound boneless short ribs
- 1½ teaspoons sea salt, divided
- ½ teaspoon freshly ground black pepper, divided
- ½ cup fresh parsley leaves
- ½ cup fresh cilantro leaves
- 1 teaspoon minced garlic
- 1 tablespoon freshly squeezed lemon juice
- ½ teaspoon ground cumin
- ¼ teaspoon red pepper flakes
- 2 tablespoons extra-virgin olive oil
- Avocado oil spray

1. Pat the short ribs dry with paper towels. Sprinkle the ribs all over with 1 teaspoon salt and ¼ teaspoon black pepper. Let sit at room temperature for 45 minutes.

2. Meanwhile, place the parsley, cilantro, garlic, lemon juice, cumin, red pepper flakes, the remaining ½ teaspoon salt, and the remaining ¼ teaspoon black pepper in a blender or food processor. With the blender running, slowly drizzle in the olive oil. Blend for about 1 minute, until the mixture is smooth and well combined.

3. Set the air fryer to 400°F. Spray both sides of the ribs with oil. Place in the basket and cook for 8 minutes. Flip and cook for another 5 minutes, until an instant-read thermometer reads 125°F for medium-rare (or to your desired doneness).

4. Allow the meat to rest for 5 to 10 minutes, then slice. Serve warm with the chimichurri sauce.

PER SERVING: Total calories: 329; Total fat: 24g; Total carbohydrates: 7g; Fiber: 1g; Erythritol: 0g; Net carbs: 6g; Protein: 21g

MACROS: 66% Fat; 26% Protein; 8% Carbs

Grilled Rib Eye Steaks with Horseradish Cream

PREP TIME: **5 MINUTES, PLUS 55 MINUTES TO REST** | COOK TIME: **10 MINUTES** | TEMPERATURE: **400°F**

While I usually don't preheat my air fryer, I have found that certain cuts of steak benefit from being cooked on an already heated surface. Preheating here yields a crust reminiscent of grilling. If you don't have a grill pan for your air fryer, the included basket will work just fine.   **SERVES 8**

KID-FRIENDLY

2 pounds rib eye steaks

Sea salt

Freshly ground black pepper

Unsalted butter, for serving

1 cup sour cream

⅓ cup heavy (whipping) cream

4 tablespoons prepared horseradish

1 teaspoon Dijon mustard

1 teaspoon apple cider vinegar

¼ teaspoon Swerve Confectioners sweetener

1. Pat the steaks dry. Season with salt and pepper and let sit at room temperature for about 45 minutes.

2. Place the grill pan in the air fryer and set the air fryer to 400°F. Let preheat for 5 minutes.

3. Working in batches, place the steaks in a single layer on the grill pan and cook for 5 minutes. Flip the steaks and cook for 5 minutes more, until an instant-read thermometer reads 120°F (or to your desired doneness).

4. Transfer the steaks to a plate and top each with a pat of butter. Tent with foil and let rest for 10 minutes.

5. Combine the sour cream, heavy cream, horseradish, Dijon mustard, vinegar, and Swerve in a bowl. Stir until smooth.

6. Serve the steaks with the horseradish cream.

PER SERVING: Total calories: 322; Total fat: 22g; Total carbohydrates: 6g; Fiber: <1g; Erythritol: <1g; Net carbs: 6g; Protein: 23g

MACROS: 61% Fat; 29% Protein; 10% Carbs

Bacon Guacamole Burgers

PREP TIME: **15 MINUTES** | COOK TIME: **9 MINUTES** | TEMPERATURE: **350°F**

This recipe brings together two of my favorite dishes in one delicious dinner! The combination of burgers and guacamole is madly addictive. I urge you to make homemade guacamole if you can. If you are pressed for time, you can purchase guacamole from the produce section and stir in bacon and cilantro for an extra punch of flavor. SERVES 8

QUICK

FAVORITE

2 pounds ground beef

2 teaspoons Taco Seasoning (page 167)

Sea salt

Freshly ground black pepper

Avocado oil spray

2 large ripe avocados, peeled and pits removed

1 tablespoon freshly squeezed lime juice

½ teaspoon ground cumin

8 ounces sliced bacon, cooked and crumbled

¼ cup chopped red onion

1 tablespoon minced garlic

1 canned chipotle chile in adobo sauce, seeded and chopped with sauce removed

1 small tomato, seeded and diced

¼ cup fresh cilantro, chopped

Lettuce leaves or keto-friendly buns, for serving

1. In a large bowl, combine the ground beef and taco seasoning. Season with salt and pepper. Mix with your hands until well-combined. Form the mixture into 8 patties, making them thinner in the center for even cooking. Spray the patties with oil.

2. Set the air fryer to 350°F. Working in batches if necessary, place the patties in the air fryer basket. Cook the burgers for 5 minutes. Flip and cook for 4 minutes more, until the patties are cooked through and an instant-read thermometer reads 160°F. Allow the burgers to rest for 5 minutes before serving.

3. Meanwhile, mash the avocados in a medium bowl. Add the lime juice and cumin. Season with salt and pepper. Stir to combine. Gently stir in the bacon, onion, garlic, chipotle chile, tomato, and cilantro. Cover with plastic wrap, gently pressing it directly on the surface of the guacamole. Refrigerate until ready to serve.

4. Top each burger with a dollop of guacamole and serve in lettuce wraps or on keto-friendly buns.

Cooking tip: I like to cook a package or two of bacon on the weekends as part of my meal prep. It makes recipes like this one come together in a flash.

PER SERVING: Total calories: 321; Total fat: 26g; Total carbohydrates: 6g; Fiber: 4g; Erythritol: 0g; Net carbs: 2g; Protein: 15g

MACROS: 73% Fat; 19% Protein; 8% Carbs

Blue Cheese Steak Salad with Balsamic-Mustard Vinaigrette

PREP TIME: **15 MINUTES, PLUS 45 MINUTES TO REST** | COOK TIME: **22 MINUTES** | TEMPERATURE: **400°F**

This recipe will make a bit more dressing than you need, and that is entirely intentional. I always reason that if I am going to go to the trouble of making a delicious homemade salad dressing, I might as well make enough so I can have another salad later in the week, too. **SERVES 4**

FAVORITE

- **2 tablespoons balsamic vinegar**
- **2 tablespoons red wine vinegar**
- **1 tablespoon Dijon mustard**
- **1 tablespoon Swerve Confectioners or keto-friendly sweetener of choice**
- **1 teaspoon minced garlic**
- **Sea salt**
- **Freshly ground black pepper**

- **¾ cup extra-virgin olive oil**
- **1 pound boneless sirloin steak**
- **Avocado oil spray**
- **1 small red onion, cut into ¼-inch-thick rounds**
- **6 ounces baby spinach**
- **½ cup cherry tomatoes, halved**
- **3 ounces blue cheese, crumbled**

1. In a blender, combine the balsamic vinegar, red wine vinegar, Dijon mustard, Swerve, and garlic. Season with salt and pepper and process until smooth. With the blender running, drizzle in the olive oil. Process until well combined. Transfer to a jar with a tight-fitting lid, and refrigerate until ready to serve (it will keep for up to 2 weeks).

2. Season the steak with salt and pepper and let sit at room temperature for at least 45 minutes, time permitting.

3. Set the air fryer to 400°F. Spray the steak with oil and place it in the air fryer basket. Cook for 6 minutes. Flip the steak and spray it with more oil. Cook for 6 minutes more for medium-rare or until the steak is done to your liking.

4. Transfer the steak to a plate, tent with a piece of aluminum foil, and allow it to rest.

5. Spray the onion slices with oil and place them in the air fryer basket. Cook at 400°F for 5 minutes. Flip the onion slices and spray them with more oil. Cook for 5 minutes more.

6. Slice the steak diagonally into thin strips. Place the spinach, cherry tomatoes, onion slices, and steak in a large bowl. Toss with the desired amount of dressing. Sprinkle with crumbled blue cheese and serve.

Variation tip: For extra flavor, try marinating the steak first. Combine ¼ cup of avocado oil, 1 tablespoon of lemon juice, 1 teaspoon of minced garlic, and ½ teaspoon of red pepper flakes in a small bowl. Season with salt and pepper and whisk to combine. Place the steak in a zip-top bag. Pour the marinade over the steak, seal the bag, and massage the marinade into the steak. Let sit at room temperature for about 1 hour or refrigerate for up to 4 hours (the lemon juice will make the meat tough if you let it marinate for longer than that).

PER SERVING: Total calories: 670; Total fat: 53g; Total carbohydrates: 9g; Fiber: 2g; Erythritol: 3g; Net carbs: 4g; Protein: 41g

MACROS: 71% Fat; 24% Protein; 5% Carbs

Parmesan-Crusted Steak

PREP TIME: **7 MINUTES, PLUS 45 MINUTES TO CHILL AND REST** | COOK TIME: **12 MINUTES** | TEMPERATURE: **400°F**

If there is anything better than cheesy, buttery steak, I don't know what it could be. The golden crust is a bit unexpected, but this is one of those crowd-pleasing recipes that everyone loves. I like to serve this steak with a simple salad of peppery arugula, lemon, and extra-virgin olive oil. **SERVES 6**

KID-FRIENDLY

5-INGREDIENT

- **½ cup (1 stick) unsalted butter, at room temperature**
- **1 cup finely grated Parmesan cheese**
- **¼ cup finely ground blanched almond flour**
- **1½ pounds New York strip steak**
- **Sea salt**
- **Freshly ground black pepper**

1. Place the butter, Parmesan cheese, and almond flour in a food processor. Process until smooth. Transfer to a sheet of parchment paper and form into a log. Wrap tightly in plastic wrap. Freeze for 45 minutes or refrigerate for at least 4 hours.

2. While the butter is chilling, season the steak liberally with salt and pepper. Let the steak rest at room temperature for about 45 minutes.

3. Place the grill pan or basket in your air fryer, set it to 400°F, and let it preheat for 5 minutes.

4. Working in batches, if necessary, place the steak on the grill pan and cook for 4 minutes. Flip and cook for 3 minutes more, until the steak is brown on both sides.

5. Remove the steak from the air fryer and arrange an equal amount of the Parmesan butter on top of each steak. Return the steak to the air fryer and continue cooking for another 5 minutes, until an instant-read thermometer reads 120°F for medium-rare and the crust is golden brown (or to your desired doneness).

6. Transfer the cooked steak to a plate; let rest for 10 minutes before serving.

Cooking tip: Keep in mind that the cooking time can vary depending on the size and thickness of your steaks. Make sure you use an instant-read thermometer for perfect steaks every time. I like the kind that allows you to leave the probe inserted in the center of the meat while it cooks and gives you an alert when it is almost done. If you are going for a well-done steak, I recommend cooking it for 5 minutes on each side before adding the Parmesan butter, to prevent over-browning.

PER SERVING: Total calories: 463; Total fat: 37g; Total carbohydrates: 2g; Fiber: 1g; Erythritol: 0g; Net carbs: 1g; Protein: 33g

MACROS: 72% Fat; 28% Protein; 0% Carbs

Steak Fajitas with Smoky Vegetables

PREP TIME: **15 MINUTES, PLUS 1 HOUR TO MARINATE** | COOK TIME: **20 TO 23 MINUTES** | TEMPERATURE: **400°F**

While the meat frequently steals the show in steak dishes, this recipe allows the vegetables to shine, too. I love how the air fryer intensifies the flavor of the peppers and onion, bringing out a touch of smokiness and a bit of sweetness. For a fun twist, I sometimes add sliced mushrooms to the mix.   SERVES 6

KID-FRIENDLY

¼ cup avocado oil

¼ cup freshly squeezed lime juice

2 teaspoons minced garlic

1 tablespoon chili powder

½ teaspoon ground cumin

Sea salt

Freshly ground black pepper

1 pound top sirloin steak or flank steak, thinly sliced against the grain

1 red bell pepper, cored, seeded, and cut into ½-inch slices

1 green bell pepper, cored, seeded, and cut into ½-inch slices

1 large onion, sliced

1. In a small bowl or blender, combine the avocado oil, lime juice, garlic, chili powder, cumin, and salt and pepper to taste.

2. Place the sliced steak in a zip-top bag or shallow dish. Place the bell peppers and onion in a separate zip-top bag or dish. Pour half the marinade over the steak and the other half over the vegetables. Seal both bags and let the steak and vegetables marinate in the refrigerator for at least 1 hour or up to 4 hours.

3. Line the air fryer basket with an air fryer liner or aluminum foil. Remove the vegetables from their bag or dish and
   shake off any excess marinade. Set the air fryer to 400°F.
   Place the vegetables in the air fryer basket and cook for
   13 minutes.

4. Remove the steak from its bag or dish and shake off any
   excess marinade. Place the steak on top of the vegetables in
   the air fryer, and cook for 7 to 10 minutes or until an
   instant-read thermometer reads 120°F for medium-rare
   (or cook to your desired doneness).

5. Serve with desired fixings, such as keto tortillas, lettuce,
   sour cream, avocado slices, shredded Cheddar cheese,
   and cilantro.

PER SERVING: Total calories: 229; Total fat: 14g; Total carbohydrates: 7g;
Fiber: 2g; Erythritol: 0g; Net carbs: 5g; Protein: 17g

MACROS: 55% Fat; 30% Protein; 15% Carbs

Goat Cheese-Stuffed Flank Steak

PREP TIME: **10 MINUTES** | COOK TIME: **14 MINUTES** | TEMPERATURE: **400°F**

Don't you love recipes where the payoff in flavor is disproportionate to the effort involved? This recipe is fancy enough for company but easy enough for a family weeknight dinner. It can be prepped (through step 5) up to 1 day ahead of time and cooked just before serving.   SERVES 6

QUICK

KID-FRIENDLY

FAVORITE

5-INGREDIENT

1 pound flank steak

1 tablespoon avocado oil

½ teaspoon sea salt

½ teaspoon garlic powder

¼ teaspoon freshly ground black pepper

2 ounces goat cheese, crumbled

1 cup baby spinach, chopped

1. Place the steak in a large zip-top bag or between two pieces of plastic wrap. Using a meat mallet or heavy-bottomed skillet, pound the steak to an even ¼-inch thickness.

2. Brush both sides of the steak with the avocado oil.

3. Mix the salt, garlic powder, and pepper in a small dish. Sprinkle this mixture over both sides of the steak.

4. Sprinkle the goat cheese over top, and top that with the spinach.

5. Starting at one of the long sides, roll the steak up tightly. Tie the rolled steak with kitchen string at 3-inch intervals.

6. Set the air fryer to 400°F. Place the steak roll-up in the air fryer basket. Cook for 7 minutes. Flip the steak and cook for an additional 7 minutes, until an instant-read thermometer reads 120°F for medium-rare (adjust the cooking time for your desired doneness).

Variation tip: Feel free to mix up the cheeses here. Mozzarella, feta, and provolone are all delicious.

PER SERVING: Total calories: 165; Total fat: 9g; Total carbohydrates: 1g; Fiber: 1g; Erythritol: 0g; Net carbs: 0g; Protein: 18g

MACROS: 49% Fat; 44% Protein; 7% Carbs

Garlic Steak

PREP TIME: **5 MINUTES, PLUS 1 HOUR TO MARINATE** | COOK TIME: **10 MINUTES** | TEMPERATURE: **400°F**

I adore garlicky goodness, and there's no better way to amp up the flavor of a steak than with a garlic marinade. I like to serve this with Roasted Brussels Sprouts with Bacon (page 41). **SERVES 6**

5-INGREDIENT

½ cup olive oil

2 tablespoons minced garlic

Sea salt

Freshly ground black pepper

1½ pounds New York strip or top sirloin steak

Unsalted butter, for serving (optional)

1. In a bowl or blender, combine the olive oil, garlic, and salt and pepper to taste.

2. Place the steak in a shallow bowl or zip-top bag. Pour the marinade over the meat, seal, and marinate in the refrigerator for at least 1 hour and up to 24 hours.

3. Place a grill pan or basket in the air fryer, set it to 400°F, and let preheat for 5 minutes.

4. Place the steak on the grill pan in a single layer, working in batches if necessary, and cook for 5 minutes. Flip the steak and cook for another 5 minutes, until an instant-read thermometer reads 120°F for medium-rare (or cook to your desired doneness).

5. Transfer the steak to a plate, and let rest for 10 minutes before serving. If desired, top the steaks with a pat of butter while they rest.

Variation tip: Try adding 1 teaspoon each of chopped rosemary, thyme, and parsley to the marinade.

PER SERVING: Total calories: 386; Total fat: 32g; Total carbohydrates: 1g; Fiber: 0g; Erythritol: 0g; Net carbs: 0g; Protein: 25g

MACROS: 74% Fat; 26% Protein; 0% Carbs

Hamburger Steaks with Onions and Mushrooms

PREP TIME: **10 MINUTES** | COOK TIME: **21 TO 23 MINUTES** | TEMPERATURE: **375°F**

This is one of those meals that I make on autopilot when I don't have a plan for dinner. It is fast and easy as it is, but if you are pressed for time, you can buy pre-sliced mushrooms. **SERVES 4**

KID-FRIENDLY

5-INGREDIENT

1 pound ground beef, formed into 4 patties

Sea salt

Freshly ground black pepper

1 cup thinly sliced onion

8 ounces mushrooms, sliced

1 tablespoon avocado oil

2 ounces Gruyère cheese, shredded (about ½ cup)

1. Season the patties on both sides with salt and pepper.

2. Set the air fryer to 375°F. Place the patties in the basket and cook for 3 minutes. Flip and cook for another 2 minutes. Remove the burgers and set aside.

3. Place the onion and mushrooms in a medium bowl. Add the avocado oil and salt and pepper to taste; toss well.

4. Place the onion and mushrooms in the air fryer basket. Cook for 15 minutes, stirring occasionally.

5. Spoon the onions and mushrooms over the patties. Top with the cheese. Place the patties back in the air fryer basket and cook for another 1 to 3 minutes, until the cheese melts and an instant-read thermometer reads 160°F. Remove and let rest. The temperature will rise to 165°F, yielding a perfect medium-well burger.

PER SERVING: Total calories: 470; Total fat: 38g; Total carbohydrates: 5g; Fiber: 1g; Erythritol: 0g; Net carbs: 4g; Protein: 25g

MACROS: 73% Fat; 21% Protein; 6% Carbs

Steak Gyro Platter

PREP TIME: **15 MINUTES, PLUS 50 MINUTES TO REST** | COOK TIME: **8 TO 10 MINUTES** | TEMPERATURE: **400°F**

Gyros are the first thing I look for at every Greek restaurant I visit. Since you can make all the elements ahead, this platter is fabulous for casual entertaining. To take flavors to the next level, add some Lemon-Garlic Mushrooms (page 39) to the plate.   **SERVES 4**

KID-FRIENDLY

FAVORITE

1 pound flank steak

1 teaspoon garlic powder

1 teaspoon ground cumin

½ teaspoon sea salt

½ teaspoon freshly ground black pepper

5 ounces shredded romaine lettuce

½ cup crumbled feta cheese

½ cup peeled and diced cucumber

⅓ cup sliced red onion

¼ cup seeded and diced tomato

2 tablespoons pitted and sliced black olives

Tzatziki Sauce (page 170), for serving

1. Pat the steak dry with paper towels. In a small bowl, combine the garlic powder, cumin, salt, and pepper. Sprinkle this mixture all over the steak, and allow the steak to rest at room temperature for 45 minutes.

2. Preheat the air fryer to 400°F. Place the steak in the air fryer basket and cook for 4 minutes. Flip the steak and cook 4 to 6 minutes more, until an instant-read thermometer reads 120°F at the thickest point for medium-rare (or as desired). Remove the steak from the air fryer and let it rest for 5 minutes.

3. Divide the romaine among plates. Top with the feta, cucumber, red onion, tomato, and olives.

4. Thinly slice the steak diagonally. Add the steak to the plates and drizzle with tzatziki sauce before serving.

PER SERVING: Total calories: 244; Total fat: 12g; Total carbohydrates: 5g; Fiber: 1g; Erythritol: 0g; Net carbs: 4g; Protein: 28g

MACROS: 44% Fat; 46% Protein; 10% Carbs

Rosemary Roast Beef

PREP TIME: **5 MINUTES, PLUS 13 HOURS TO MARINATE AND REST** | COOK TIME: **30 TO 35 MINUTES** | TEMPERATURE: **325°F**

The air fryer makes cooking a large cut of meat so fast and easy. This tasty roast is perfect for preparing on Sunday for easy meals throughout the week. Remember that my go-to air fryer is an XXL model, so it will fit a 2-pound roast. If you're using a smaller model, choose as large a roast as your air fryer can fit—just make sure you use an instant-read meat thermometer and adjust your cooking time accordingly. **SERVES 8**

KID-FRIENDLY

FAVORITE

5-INGREDIENT

1 (2-pound) top round beef roast, tied with kitchen string

Sea salt

Freshly ground black pepper

2 teaspoons minced garlic

2 tablespoons finely chopped fresh rosemary

¼ cup avocado oil

1. Season the roast generously with salt and pepper.

2. In a small bowl, whisk together the garlic, rosemary, and avocado oil. Rub this all over the roast. Cover loosely with aluminum foil or plastic wrap and refrigerate for at least 12 hours or up to 2 days.

3. Remove the roast from the refrigerator and allow to sit at room temperature for about 1 hour.

4. Set the air fryer to 325°F. Place the roast in the air fryer basket and cook for 15 minutes. Flip the roast and cook for 15 to 20 minutes more, until the meat is browned and an instant-read thermometer reads 120°F at the thickest part (for medium-rare).

5. Transfer the meat to a cutting board, and let it rest for 15 minutes before thinly slicing and serving.

PER SERVING: Total calories: 213; Total fat: 10g; Total carbohydrates: 2g; Fiber: <1g; Erythritol: 0g; Net carbs: 2g; Protein: 25g

MACROS: 42% Fat; 47% Protein; 11% Carbs

Tenderloin with Crispy Shallots

PREP TIME: **5 MINUTES, PLUS 45 MINUTES TO REST** | COOK TIME: **18 TO 20 MINUTES** | TEMPERATURE: **400°F, THEN 300°F**

I love a restaurant-quality meal that requires barely any work. A good tenderloin steak doesn't need anything more than salt and pepper, but the addition of shallots makes this spectacular. The total cooking time will be largely dependent on the size and thickness of your steaks. I can't recommend an instant-read thermometer enough here. **SERVES 6**

5-INGREDIENT

1½ pounds beef tenderloin steaks

Sea salt

Freshly ground black pepper

4 medium shallots

1 teaspoon olive oil or avocado oil

1. Season both sides of the steaks with salt and pepper, and let them sit at room temperature for 45 minutes.

2. Set the air fryer to 400°F and let it preheat for 5 minutes.

3. Working in batches if necessary, place the steaks in the air fryer basket in a single layer and cook for 5 minutes. Flip and cook for 5 minutes longer, until an instant-read thermometer inserted in the center of the steaks registers 120°F for medium-rare (or as desired). Remove the steaks and tent with aluminum foil to rest.

4. Set the air fryer to 300°F. In a medium bowl, toss the shallots with the oil. Place the shallots in the basket and cook for 5 minutes, then give them a toss and cook for 3 to 5 minutes more, until crispy and golden brown.

5. Place the steaks on serving plates and arrange the shallots on top.

PER SERVING: Total calories: 186; Total fat: 5g; Total carbohydrates: 5g; Fiber: 0g; Erythritol: 0g; Net carbs: 5g; Protein: 30g

MACROS: 24% Fat; 65% Protein; 11% Carbs

Sesame Beef Lettuce Tacos

PREP TIME: **15 MINUTES, PLUS 2 HOURS TO MARINATE** | COOK TIME: **8 TO 10 MINUTES** | TEMPERATURE: **400°F**

It is easy to fall into ruts with food, and a little variety, such as these lettuce tacos, infuses everyday meals with excitement. With two teenage boys, flank steak has started to make a regular appearance on our table; it is a less expensive cut that benefits from marinating. You will be surprised at just how much flavor this simple dish boasts. **SERVES 4**

KID-FRIENDLY

¼ cup coconut aminos

¼ cup avocado oil

2 tablespoons cooking sherry

1 tablespoon brown sugar substitute, such as Swerve or Sukrin Gold

1 tablespoon ground cumin

1 teaspoon minced garlic

Sea salt

Freshly ground black pepper

1 pound flank steak

8 butter lettuce leaves

2 scallions, sliced

1 tablespoon toasted sesame seeds (see Cooking tip)

Hot sauce, for serving

Lime wedges, for serving

Flaky sea salt (optional)

1. In a small bowl, whisk together the coconut aminos, avocado oil, cooking sherry, brown sugar substitute, cumin, garlic, and salt and pepper to taste.

2. Place the steak in a shallow dish. Pour the marinade over the beef. Cover the dish with plastic wrap and let it marinate in the refrigerator for at least 2 hours or overnight.

3. Remove the flank steak from the dish and discard the marinade.

4. Set the air fryer to 400°F. Place the steak in the air fryer basket and cook for 4 to 6 minutes. Flip the steak and cook for 4 minutes more, until an instant-read thermometer reads 120°F at the thickest part (or cook it to your desired doneness). Allow the steak to rest for 10 minutes, then slice it thinly against the grain.

5. Stack 2 lettuce leaves on top of each other and add some sliced meat. Top with scallions and sesame seeds. Drizzle with hot sauce and lime juice, and finish with a little flaky salt (if using). Repeat with the remaining lettuce leaves and fillings.

Cooking tip: To toast sesame seeds, heat a dry skillet over medium heat. Place the sesame seeds in the skillet and cook for about 3 minutes, stirring occasionally. The sesame seeds are done when they are lightly browned. Be sure to watch them carefully to avoid scorching.

PER SERVING: Total calories: 349; Total fat: 22g; Total carbohydrates: 10g; Fiber: 2g; Erythritol: 3g; Net carbs: 5g; Protein: 25g

MACROS: 57% Fat; 29% Protein; 14% Carbs

Chipotle Taco Pizzas

PREP TIME: **25 MINUTES** | COOK TIME: **36 MINUTES** | TEMPERATURE: **375°F**

This taco pizza is delicious on its own, but perhaps even more so when sprinkled with pickled jalapeños, tomatoes, lettuce, and cilantro after cooking. I like to use a medium-heat salsa, but feel free to use whatever level of spiciness works for your family.   **SERVES 6**

KID-FRIENDLY

FAVORITE

1 recipe Fathead Pizza Dough (page 171)

1 pound ground beef

2 tablespoons Taco Seasoning (page 167)

1 canned chipotle chile in adobo sauce, diced and sauce removed

⅓ cup plus 1 tablespoon sugar-free salsa, divided

6 ounces Cheddar cheese, grated

3 scallions, chopped

¼ cup sour cream

1. Divide the dough into three equal pieces. Place each piece between two sheets of parchment paper, and roll it into a 7-inch round. Place one dough round in a 7-inch cake pan or air fryer pizza pan (or a similar pan that fits inside your air fryer). Place the pan in the air fryer basket.

2. Set your air fryer to 375°F. Cook the dough for 6 minutes. Remove from the air fryer and repeat with the remaining dough.

3. While the crusts are cooking, heat a large skillet over medium-high heat. Add the ground beef and cook, breaking the meat up with a spoon, for 5 minutes. Stir in the taco seasoning and chipotle chile, and cook until the meat is browned. Remove the skillet from the heat and stir in ⅓ cup of salsa.

4. Divide the meat among the pizza crusts. Top with the cheese and scallions. Return one pizza to the air fryer and cook for 6 minutes, until the cheese is melted. Repeat with the remaining pizzas.

5. Combine the sour cream and remaining 1 tablespoon of salsa in a small bowl. Drizzle this over the finished pizzas.

6. If desired, top the pizzas with additional desired toppings, such as shredded romaine lettuce, pickled jalapeño slices, diced tomatoes, cilantro, and lime juice. Serve warm.

Cooking tip: While the crusts can be made and baked up to a few days ahead of time, I recommend waiting to top the pizzas until just before serving to avoid the crusts becoming soggy. Leftovers taste great, but you will lose the crispiness of the crust.

PER SERVING: Total calories: 614; Total fat: 52g; Total carbohydrates: 10g; Fiber: 4g; Erythritol: 0g; Net carbs: 6g; Protein: 34g

MACROS: 76% Fat; 22% Protein; 2% Carbs

Beef Empanadas

PREP TIME: 20 MINUTES | **COOK TIME: 24 TO 27 MINUTES** | **TEMPERATURE: 400°F**

I am perfectly content eating appetizers for dinner—in fact, I've said for years that they are the best part of the meal. These empanadas are ridiculously flavorful and surprisingly easy to throw together. They are also great to grab for on-the-go lunches or quick snacks on the weekend when everyone is coming and going from various activities.   **SERVES 10**

FAVORITE

1 tablespoon unsalted butter

½ medium onion, chopped

2 teaspoons minced garlic

½ pound ground beef

2 teaspoons ground cumin

1 teaspoon smoked paprika

⅛ teaspoon cayenne pepper (more or less to taste)

Sea salt

Freshly ground black pepper

½ cup keto-friendly tomato sauce

1 recipe Fathead Pizza Dough (page 171)

½ cup shredded sharp Cheddar cheese

1. Heat the butter over medium-high heat in a large skillet. Once the butter is melted and hot, add the onion and cook, stirring occasionally, for about 6 minutes or until soft. Stir in the garlic and sauté for 1 minute.

2. Add the ground beef and cook, breaking the meat up with a spoon, until browned, about 5 minutes. Stir in the cumin, paprika, cayenne pepper, and salt and black pepper to taste, and cook for 2 minutes. Stir in the tomato sauce. Bring to a boil and then reduce the heat to a simmer. Cook for 3 minutes, then remove the skillet from the heat.

3. Line a baking sheet with parchment paper.

4. On another sheet of parchment paper, roll out the dough to about the size of your baking sheet. Use a 3½- or 3¾-inch round cookie cutter to cut the dough into rounds. Ball up the scraps, roll them out again, and cut more rounds until all the dough has been used.

5. Transfer the rounds to a clean sheet of parchment paper. Place about ½ tablespoon of ground beef filling in the center of each round. Top with a sprinkle of Cheddar cheese. Fold the dough in half over the filling, using a fork to seal the edges together.

6. Set the air fryer to 400°F. Working in batches if needed, place the empanadas in the air fryer basket in a single layer. Cook for 7 to 10 minutes, until golden brown.

PER SERVING: Total calories: 250; Total fat: 21g; Total carbohydrates: 5g; Fiber: 2g; Erythritol: 0g; Net carbs: 3g; Protein: 13g

MACROS: 76% Fat; 21% Protein; 3% Carbs

New York Strips with Walnut–Blue Cheese Butter

PREP TIME: **15 MINUTES, PLUS 2 HOURS TO CHILL THE BUTTER** | COOK TIME: **10 MINUTES** | TEMPERATURE: **400°F**

I first had a steak topped with walnut–blue cheese butter more than 20 years ago in a little restaurant in Atlanta. It was the type of place where you sit outside under twinkling lights and share a bottle of wine with friends. Since then, this flavor combination has held a special place in my heart, the earthy walnuts contrasting perfectly with the sharp cheese. This is one recipe you will want to make again and again.   SERVES 6

FAVORITE

½ cup unsalted butter, at room temperature

½ cup crumbled blue cheese

2 tablespoons finely chopped walnuts

1 tablespoon minced fresh rosemary

1 teaspoon minced garlic

¼ teaspoon cayenne pepper

Sea salt

Freshly ground black pepper

1½ pounds New York strip steaks, at room temperature

1. In a medium bowl, combine the butter, blue cheese, walnuts, rosemary, garlic, and cayenne pepper and salt and black pepper to taste. Use clean hands to ensure that everything is well combined. Place the mixture on a sheet of parchment paper and form it into a log. Wrap it tightly in plastic wrap. Refrigerate for at least 2 hours or freeze for 30 minutes.

2. Season the steaks generously with salt and pepper.

3. Place the air fryer basket or grill pan in the air fryer. Set the air fryer to 400°F and let it preheat for 5 minutes.

4. Place the steaks in the basket in a single layer and cook for 5 minutes. Flip the steaks, and cook for 5 minutes more, until an instant-read thermometer reads 120°F for medium-rare (or as desired).

5. Transfer the steaks to a plate. Cut the butter into pieces and place the desired amount on top of the steaks. Tent a piece of aluminum foil over the steaks and allow to sit for 10 minutes before serving.

6. Store any remaining butter in a sealed container in the refrigerator for up to 2 weeks.

Substitution tip: Feel free to use any cut of meat you like here. Rib eye and sirloin steaks are particularly good.

PER SERVING: Total calories: 418; Total fat: 34g; Total carbohydrates: 1g; Fiber: <1g; Erythritol: 0g; Net carbs: 1g; Protein: 28g

MACROS: 73% Fat; 27% Protein; 0% Carbs

Sausage-Stuffed Peppers, page 129

7

Pork

Pork Adobo

PREP TIME: **15 MINUTES, PLUS 8 HOURS TO MARINATE** | COOK TIME: **10 TO 14 MINUTES** | TEMPERATURE: **400°F**

My youngest son fearlessly eats all my kitchen experiments, yet even I was surprised by how much he loved this recipe. It has a punchy flavor that is a tad unexpected. If you don't like heat, feel free to leave out the serrano chile. **SERVES 6**

FAVORITE

⅓ cup coconut aminos

⅓ cup white vinegar

¼ cup avocado oil

2 tablespoons brown sugar substitute, such as Swerve or Sukrin Gold

2 teaspoons minced garlic

Salt

Freshly ground black pepper

3 bay leaves

1 serrano chile, stemmed and halved lengthwise

1¼ pounds (1-inch-thick) boneless pork chops

Avocado oil spray

1. In a small bowl, combine the coconut aminos, vinegar, avocado oil, brown sugar substitute, and garlic. Season with salt and pepper. Whisk until the sugar substitute dissolves. Transfer half of the sauce to a separate container; cover and set aside until ready to serve. To the bowl with the remaining sauce, add the bay leaves and serrano chile.

2. Place the pork chops in a shallow dish, and pour the marinade with serrano chile over top. Cover the dish with plastic wrap and let the pork marinate in the refrigerator for 8 hours or overnight.

3. Remove the pork from the dish and discard the marinade. Spray the pork chops with oil.

4. Set the air fryer to 400°F. Place the pork chops in a single layer in the air fryer basket. Cook for 6 minutes. Flip the chops and spray them with more oil. Cook for 4 to 8 minutes more, until an instant-read thermometer reads 145°F.

5. While the pork cooks, pour the reserved sauce into a small saucepan over medium heat. Bring to a simmer and cook for about 5 minutes, until the liquid is syrupy and reduced by half.

6. Remove the pork from the air fryer and allow it to rest for 5 minutes. Cut the pork into bite-size pieces and serve with the sauce.

Cooking tip: Make sure you don't overdo the salt, since the coconut aminos add a nice salty touch to the meat.

PER SERVING: Total calories: 218; Total fat: 14g; Total carbohydrates: 7g; Fiber: <1g; Erythritol: 4g; Net carbs: 3g; Protein: 18g

MACROS: 58% Fat; 33% Protein; 9% Carbs

Cream Cheese Sausage Balls

PREP TIME: **10 MINUTES** | COOK TIME: **10 MINUTES** | TEMPERATURE: **350°F**

I make this recipe all the time. They freeze beautifully and are perfect to have on hand in the event of unexpected guests. To cook them from frozen, just add 5 minutes to the cooking time.   SERVES 12

QUICK

KID-FRIENDLY

FAVORITE

1¾ cups finely ground blanched almond flour

1 tablespoon baking powder

½ teaspoon sea salt

¼ teaspoon freshly ground black pepper

¼ teaspoon cayenne pepper

1 pound fresh pork sausage, casings removed, crumbled

8 ounces Cheddar cheese, shredded

8 ounces cream cheese, at room temperature, cut into chunks

1. In a large mixing bowl, combine the almond flour, baking powder, salt, black pepper, and cayenne pepper.

2. Add the sausage, Cheddar cheese, and cream cheese. Stir to combine, and then, using clean hands, mix until all of the ingredients are well incorporated.

3. Form the mixture into 1½-inch balls.

4. Set the air fryer to 350°F. Arrange the sausage balls in a single layer in the air fryer basket, working in batches if necessary. Cook for 5 minutes. Flip the sausage balls and cook for 5 minutes more.

Cooking tip: To freeze, arrange the uncooked balls on a parchment paper–lined baking sheet and cover with foil. Freeze for 4 hours, then transfer to a zip-top freezer bag or other container and return them to the freezer.

Substitution tip: Feel free to use turkey or chicken sausage in place of the pork.

PER SERVING: Total calories: 386; Total fat: 27g; Total carbohydrates: 5g; Fiber: 2g; Erythritol: 0g; Net carbs: 3g; Protein: 16g

MACROS: 63% Fat; 17% Protein; 20% Carbs

Sausage-Stuffed Peppers

PREP TIME: **15 MINUTES** | COOK TIME: **28 TO 30 MINUTES** | TEMPERATURE: **350°F**

Stuffed peppers can easily be made ahead if you meal prep, making them a super-convenient weeknight meal. This recipe isn't particularly fussy, so feel free to improvise with whatever you have on hand. Serve these with an Italian green salad for a complete meal.   **SERVES 6**

KID-FRIENDLY

Avocado oil spray

8 ounces Italian sausage, casings removed

½ cup chopped mushrooms

¼ cup diced onion

1 teaspoon Italian seasoning

Sea salt

Freshly ground black pepper

1 cup keto-friendly marinara sauce

3 bell peppers, halved and seeded

3 ounces provolone cheese, shredded

1. Spray a large skillet with oil and place it over medium-high heat. Add the sausage and cook for 5 minutes, breaking up the meat with a wooden spoon. Add the mushrooms, onion, and Italian seasoning, and season with salt and pepper. Cook for 5 minutes more. Stir in the marinara sauce and cook until heated through.

2. Scoop the sausage filling into the bell pepper halves.

3. Set the air fryer to 350°F. Arrange the peppers in a single layer in the air fryer basket, working in batches if necessary. Cook for 15 minutes.

4. Top the stuffed peppers with the cheese and cook for 3 to 5 minutes more, until the cheese is melted and the peppers are tender.

PER SERVING: Total calories: 186; Total fat: 12g; Total carbohydrates: 8g; Fiber: 2g; Erythritol: 0g; Net carbs: 6g; Protein: 11g

MACROS: 58% Fat; 24% Protein; 18% Carbs

Pork Kebabs

PREP TIME: **15 MINUTES, PLUS 2 HOURS TO MARINATE** | COOK TIME: **6 TO 8 MINUTES** | TEMPERATURE: **375°F**

Although you do have to plan ahead to allow time for the pork to marinate, the hands-on time is limited here. I love the tangy sweetness that the ginger ale brings to this marinade.   SERVES 4

KID-FRIENDLY

¼ cup coconut aminos

¼ cup sugar-free ketchup

2 tablespoons freshly squeezed lime juice

2 tablespoons brown sugar substitute, such as Swerve or Sukrin Gold

1 teaspoon minced garlic

Sea salt

Freshly ground black pepper

1 cup stevia-sweetened ginger ale, such as Zevia brand (optional)

1 pound pork tenderloin, cut into 1½-inch cubes

1 red bell pepper, cut into 1½-inch pieces

1 small red onion, cut into 1½-inch pieces

1. In a small bowl, whisk together the coconut aminos, ketchup, lime juice, brown sugar substitute, garlic, and salt and pepper to taste. Whisk in the ginger ale (if using).

2. Place the pork in a shallow dish and pour the marinade over top. Cover the dish with plastic wrap and let the pork marinate in the refrigerator for 2 to 4 hours.

3. Thread the marinated pork cubes, red bell pepper, and onion on skewers, alternating as you go.

4. Set the air fryer to 375°F. Place the kebabs in the air fryer basket in a single layer and cook for 6 to 8 minutes, until an instant-read thermometer reads 145°F.

Cooking tip: If you are using wooden skewers, soak them in water for at least 30 minutes before cooking. If you skip the ginger ale, whisk ½ cup of avocado oil into the marinade.

PER SERVING: Total calories: 271; Total fat: 9g; Total carbohydrates: 14g; Fiber: 1g; Erythritol: 6g; Net carbs: 7g; Protein: 34g

MACROS: 30% Fat; 50% Protein; 20% Carbs

Bacon Wedge Salad

PREP TIME: **10 MINUTES** | COOK TIME: **10 TO 13 MINUTES** | TEMPERATURE: **400°F**

This salad is a classic, and perfect for serving with steak or a juicy burger. I've added pecans for an extra boost of texture. If you really want the flavors to pop, add some Sweet and Spicy Pecans (page 40) to the finished salad.   **SERVES 4**

QUICK

8 ounces bacon, sliced

1 head iceberg lettuce

6 ounces blue cheese crumbles

½ cup pecans, chopped

8 cherry tomatoes, halved

1 recipe Blue Cheese Dressing (page 169)

1. Set the air fryer to 400°F. Arrange the bacon strips in a single layer in the air fryer basket (some overlapping is okay because the bacon will shrink as it cooks, but work in batches if necessary). Cook for 8 minutes. Flip the bacon and cook for 2 to 5 minutes more, until the bacon is crisp. The total cooking time will depend on the thickness of your bacon.

2. Cut the iceberg lettuce into 8 wedges and place 2 wedges on each of 4 serving plates.

3. Crumble the bacon and scatter it and the blue cheese crumbles, chopped pecans, and cherry tomatoes over the lettuce.

4. Spoon the desired amount of dressing onto each wedge so it drips down the sides.

PER SERVING: Total calories: 900; Total fat: 85g; Total carbohydrates: 12g; Fiber: 3g; Erythritol: 0g; Net carbs: 9g; Protein: 27g

MACROS: 85% Fat; 12% Protein; 3% Carbs

Sausage and Spinach Calzones

PREP TIME: **20 MINUTES** | COOK TIME: **18 TO 24 MINUTES** | TEMPERATURE: **325°F**

These calzones are full of indulgent flavors and are easier to make than you might think. Feel free to adapt these using different vegetables and cheeses. **SERVES 4**

FAVORITE

Avocado oil spray

5 ounces Italian sausage, casings removed

1 teaspoon minced garlic

3 ounces baby spinach, chopped

½ cup ricotta cheese

½ cup shredded mozzarella cheese

¼ cup grated Parmesan cheese

½ teaspoon red pepper flakes

Sea salt

Freshly ground black pepper

1 recipe Fathead Pizza Dough (page 171)

Keto-friendly marinara sauce, for serving

1. Spray a skillet with oil and heat it over medium-high heat. Put the sausage in the skillet and cook for 5 minutes, breaking up the meat with a spoon. Add the garlic and spinach and cook until the spinach wilts, 2 to 3 minutes. Remove the skillet from the heat.

2. Stir together the ricotta, mozzarella, Parmesan, red pepper flakes, and the sausage-spinach mixture in a large bowl. Season with salt and pepper.

3. Divide the pizza dough into 4 equal pieces and roll each into a 6-inch round. Spoon one-fourth of the filling onto the center of each round. Fold the dough over the filling and use the back of a fork to seal the edges closed.

4. Set the air fryer to 325°F. Place the calzones in a single layer in the basket, working in batches if necessary. Cook for 11 to 15 minutes, until golden brown. Serve warm with marinara sauce.

PER SERVING: Total calories: 564; Total fat: 46g; Total carbohydrates: 11g; Fiber: 5g; Erythritol: 0g; Net carbs: 6g; Protein: 35g

MACROS: 73% Fat; 25% Protein; 2% Carbs

Parmesan-Breaded Boneless Pork Chops

PREP TIME: **15 MINUTES** | COOK TIME: **9 TO 14 MINUTES** | TEMPERATURE: **400°F**

These breaded pork chops are super-quick to make and totally delicious. You can even use finely crushed pork rinds instead of the almond flour for the breading. I like to serve these chops with Spicy Roasted Broccoli (page 50) or Cabbage Wedges with Caraway Butter (page 46). **SERVES 4**

QUICK

KID-FRIENDLY

2 large eggs

½ cup finely grated Parmesan cheese

½ cup finely ground blanched almond flour or finely crushed pork rinds

1 teaspoon paprika

½ teaspoon dried oregano

½ teaspoon garlic powder

Salt

Freshly ground black pepper

1¼ pounds (1-inch-thick) boneless pork chops

Avocado oil spray

1. Beat the eggs in a shallow bowl. In a separate bowl, combine the Parmesan cheese, almond flour, paprika, oregano, garlic powder, and salt and pepper to taste.

2. Dip the pork chops into the eggs, then coat them with the Parmesan mixture, gently pressing the coating onto the meat. Spray the breaded pork chops with oil.

3. Set the air fryer to 400°F. Place the pork chops in the air fryer basket in a single layer, working in batches if necessary. Cook for 6 minutes. Flip the chops and spray them with more oil. Cook for another 3 to 8 minutes, until an instant-read thermometer reads 145°F.

4. Allow the pork chops to rest for at least 5 minutes, then serve.

Cooking tip: If you have thicker pork chops, increase the cooking time. Two-inch-thick chops will take about 20 minutes total to cook through.

PER SERVING: Total calories: 351; Total fat: 20g; Total carbohydrates: 4g; Fiber: 2g; Erythritol: 0g; Net carbs: 2g; Protein: 38g

MACROS: 51% Fat; 43% Protein; 6% Carbs

Italian Sausage with Peppers and Onion

PREP TIME: **10 MINUTES** | COOK TIME: **24 MINUTES** | TEMPERATURE: **400°F**

Sausage, peppers, and onions are a delightful meal on their own—it's an Italian classic for a reason. If you like, toss them with ½ cup of sugar-free marinara sauce; my go-to brand is Rao's Homemade®. To add something green to your meal, serve Buttery Green Beans (page 51) on the side. **SERVES 4**

5-INGREDIENT

1 bell pepper (any color), sliced

1 medium onion, sliced

1 tablespoon avocado oil

1 teaspoon Italian seasoning

Sea salt

Freshly ground black pepper

1 pound Italian sausage links

1. Place the bell pepper and onion in a medium bowl, and toss with the avocado oil, Italian seasoning, and salt and pepper to taste.

2. Set the air fryer to 400°F. Put the vegetables in the air fryer basket and cook for 12 minutes.

3. Push the vegetables to the side of the basket and arrange the sausage links in the bottom of the basket in a single layer. Spoon the vegetables over the sausages. Cook for 12 minutes, tossing halfway through, until an instant-read thermometer inserted into the sausage reads 160°F.

Cooking tip: If your air fryer tends to smoke when cooking bacon or sausage, try adding an air fryer parchment liner.

PER SERVING: Total calories: 339; Total fat: 27g; Total carbohydrates: 5g; Fiber: 1g; Erythritol: 0g; Net carbs: 4g; Protein: 17g

MACROS: 72% Fat; 20% Protein; 8% Carbs

Bone-In Pork Chops

PREP TIME: **5 MINUTES** | COOK TIME: **10 TO 12 MINUTES** | TEMPERATURE: **400°F**

When you are craving something simple that never fails to delight, these pork chops are a must. I love the heat from the cayenne pepper and smoked paprika, but feel free to leave both spices out if you are sensitive to spice. Serve these chops with cauliflower rice and Lemon-Thyme Asparagus (page 48) or Spicy Roasted Broccoli (page 50). **SERVES 2**

QUICK

5-INGREDIENT

1 pound bone-in pork chops

1 tablespoon avocado oil

1 teaspoon smoked paprika

½ teaspoon onion powder

¼ teaspoon cayenne pepper

Sea salt

Freshly ground black pepper

1. Brush the pork chops with the avocado oil. In a small dish, mix together the smoked paprika, onion powder, cayenne pepper, and salt and black pepper to taste. Sprinkle the seasonings over both sides of the pork chops.

2. Set the air fryer to 400°F. Place the chops in the air fryer basket in a single layer, working in batches if necessary. Cook for 10 to 12 minutes, until an instant-read thermometer reads 145°F at the chops' thickest point.

3. Remove the chops from the air fryer and allow them to rest for 5 minutes before serving.

Cooking tip: For extra flavor, try brining the pork chops before seasoning and cooking them. To do this, combine 2 cups warm water with ¼ cup sea salt. Stir to dissolve the salt, then add 1 cup of cold water. Pour this over the pork chops in an airtight container. Cover and refrigerate for at least 1 hour or overnight, then drain.

PER SERVING: Total calories: 344; Total fat: 21g; Total carbohydrates: 2g; Fiber: <1g; Erythritol: 0g; Net carbs: 2g; Protein: 33g

MACROS: 55% Fat; 38% Protein; 7% Carbs

Sausage and Cauliflower Arancini

PREP TIME: **20 MINUTES, PLUS 30 MINUTES TO CHILL** | COOK TIME: **28 TO 32 MINUTES** | TEMPERATURE: **400°F**

I have always had a weakness for arancini—rice balls that are traditionally deep-fried—and I can't get enough of these delicious little morsels! In place of the traditional rice, I use riced cauliflower. These "rice" balls are crispy, cheesy, and make a great appetizer—or you can serve them with a salad for a complete meal. Try them once, and, like me, you'll be addicted. **SERVES 6**

FAVORITE

Avocado oil spray

6 ounces Italian sausage, casings removed

¼ cup diced onion

1 teaspoon minced garlic

1 teaspoon dried thyme

Sea salt

Freshly ground black pepper

2½ cups cauliflower rice

3 ounces cream cheese

4 ounces Cheddar cheese, shredded

1 large egg

½ cup finely ground blanched almond flour

¼ cup finely grated Parmesan cheese

Keto-friendly marinara sauce, for serving

1. Spray a large skillet with oil and place it over medium-high heat. Once the skillet is hot, put the sausage in the skillet and cook for 7 minutes, breaking up the meat with the back of a spoon.

2. Reduce the heat to medium and add the onion. Cook for 5 minutes, then add the garlic, thyme, and salt and pepper to taste. Cook for 1 minute more.

3. Add the cauliflower rice and cream cheese to the skillet. Cook for 7 minutes, stirring frequently, until the cream cheese melts and the cauliflower is tender.

4. Remove the skillet from the heat and stir in the Cheddar cheese. Using a cookie scoop, form the mixture into 1½-inch balls. Place the balls on a parchment paper–lined baking sheet. Freeze for 30 minutes.

5. Place the egg in a shallow bowl and beat it with a fork. In a separate bowl, stir together the almond flour and Parmesan cheese.

6. Dip the cauliflower balls into the egg, then coat them with the almond flour mixture, gently pressing the mixture to the balls to adhere.

7. Set the air fryer to 400°F. Spray the cauliflower rice balls with oil, and arrange them in a single layer in the air fryer basket, working in batches if necessary. Cook for 5 minutes. Flip the rice balls and spray them with more oil. Cook for 3 to 7 minutes longer, until the balls are golden brown.

8. Serve warm with marinara sauce.

PER SERVING: Total calories: 290; Total fat: 23g; Total carbohydrates: 6g; Fiber: 2g; Erythritol: 0g; Net carbs: 4g; Protein: 15g

MACROS: 71% Fat; 21% Protein; 8% Carbs

Bacon-Wrapped Vegetable Kebabs

PREP TIME: **10 MINUTES** | COOK TIME: **10 TO 12 MINUTES** | TEMPERATURE: **400°F**

These veggie kebabs make for a fast and easy side that is anything but boring. Bacon fat seasons the vegetables as they cook, making them ridiculously delectable. Feel free to mix up the vegetables here and use whatever you have on hand. These are great as an appetizer or lunch, and perfect for taking to a potluck or summer barbecue.   **SERVES 4**

QUICK

5-INGREDIENT

4 ounces mushrooms, sliced

1 small zucchini, sliced

12 grape tomatoes

4 ounces sliced bacon, halved

Avocado oil spray

Sea salt

Freshly ground black pepper

Garlic Ranch Dressing (page 168), for serving

1. Stack 3 mushroom slices, 1 zucchini slice, and 1 grape tomato. Wrap a bacon strip around the vegetables and thread them onto a skewer. Repeat with the remaining vegetables and bacon. Spray with oil and sprinkle with salt and pepper.

2. Set the air fryer to 400°F. Place the skewers in the air fryer basket in a single layer, working in batches if necessary, and cook for 5 minutes. Flip the skewers and cook for 5 to 7 minutes more, until the bacon is crispy and the vegetables are tender.

3. Serve with Garlic Ranch Dressing.

PER SERVING: Total calories: 73; Total fat: 4g; Total carbohydrates: 4g; Fiber: 1g; Erythritol: 0g; Net carbs: 3g; Protein: 6g

MACROS: 49% Fat; 33% Protein; 18% Carbs

Ricotta and Sausage Pizzas

PREP TIME: **15 MINUTES** | COOK TIME: **30 TO 42 MINUTES** | TEMPERATURE: **375°F**

Pizza is a weeknight standard around our house, and this is one of our favorites. For a fun twist, add some briny olives, roasted red peppers, roasted garlic, and red pepper flakes. It's also fun to let the kids put together their own pizzas. Just lay out all the ingredients and let them do the work! **SERVES 6**

KID-FRIENDLY

1 recipe Fathead Pizza Dough (page 171)

6 ounces Italian sausage, casings removed

⅓ cup sugar-free marinara sauce

3 ounces low-moisture mozzarella cheese, shredded

½ small red onion, thinly sliced

3 tablespoons ricotta cheese

1. Divide the dough into 3 equal pieces. Working with one at a time, place a dough piece between 2 sheets of parchment paper and roll it into a 7-inch round. Place the dough in a 7-inch cake pan or pizza pan.

2. Set the air fryer to 375°F. Place the pan in the air fryer basket and cook for 6 minutes. Repeat with the remaining dough rounds.

3. While the crusts cook, place a medium skillet over medium-high heat. Once the skillet is hot, put the sausage in the skillet and cook, breaking it up with the back of a spoon, for 8 to 10 minutes, until the meat is browned and cooked through.

4. Spread the marinara sauce on the pizza crusts. Top with the mozzarella, cooked sausage, and onion slices. Dollop with the ricotta cheese.

5. Set the air fryer to 375°F. Cooking one at a time, place the pizzas in the air fryer basket and cook for 4 to 8 more minutes, until the cheese melts.

PER SERVING: Total calories: 365; Total fat: 29g; Total carbohydrates: 8g; Fiber: 3g; Erythritol: 0g; Net carbs: 5g; Protein: 22g

MACROS: 72% Fat; 24% Protein; 4% Carbs

Sausage and Pork Meatballs

PREP TIME: **15 MINUTES** | COOK TIME: **8 TO 12 MINUTES** | TEMPERATURE: **400°F**

We love big flavors in our family, and these meatballs really deliver. I like to use hot Italian sausage for an extra kick, but sweet sausage works well, too, and makes this recipe kid-friendly. If you don't have gelatin on hand, feel free to omit it. It helps with the texture, but isn't necessary.   **SERVES 8**

QUICK

KID-FRIENDLY

FAVORITE

1 large egg

1 teaspoon gelatin

1 pound ground pork

½ pound Italian sausage, casings removed, crumbled

⅓ cup Parmesan cheese

¼ cup finely diced onion

1 tablespoon tomato paste

1 teaspoon minced garlic

1 teaspoon dried oregano

¼ teaspoon red pepper flakes

Sea salt

Freshly ground black pepper

Keto-friendly marinara sauce, for serving

1. Beat the egg in a small bowl and sprinkle with the gelatin. Allow to sit for 5 minutes.

2. In a large bowl, combine the ground pork, sausage, Parmesan, onion, tomato paste, garlic, oregano, and red pepper flakes. Season with salt and black pepper.

3. Stir the gelatin mixture, then add it to the other ingredients and, using clean hands, mix to ensure that everything is well combined. Form into 1½-inch round meatballs.

4. Set the air fryer to 400°F. Place the meatballs in the air fryer basket in a single layer, cooking in batches as needed. Cook for 5 minutes. Flip and cook for 3 to 7 minutes more, or until an instant-read thermometer reads 160°F.

PER SERVING: Total calories: 254; Total fat: 20g; Total carbohydrates: 1g; Fiber: <1g; Erythritol: 0g; Net carbs: 1g; Protein: 17g

MACROS: 71% Fat; 27% Protein; 2% Carbs

Herbed Pork Tenderloin

PREP TIME: **5 MINUTES** | COOK TIME: **16 TO 21 MINUTES** | TEMPERATURE: **400°F**

When you need a fast meal, this never fails to be a hit. It's also fantastic for meal prepping, since you can use the meat throughout the week for lunches, low-carb wraps, or a repeat dinner when you just want a break from cooking.　**SERVES 6**

QUICK

KID-FRIENDLY

2 pounds pork tenderloin, trimmed of fat and halved crosswise

¼ cup avocado oil

1 tablespoon Swerve Confectioners or other keto-friendly sweetener

2 teaspoons dried sage

1 teaspoon dried parsley

1 teaspoon dried rosemary

1 teaspoon dried thyme

1 teaspoon dried oregano

1 teaspoon freshly ground black pepper

1 teaspoon sea salt

1. Pierce the tenderloin all over with a fork.

2. In a small bowl, whisk together the avocado oil, Swerve, sage, parsley, rosemary, thyme, oregano, pepper, and salt. Rub the mixture all over the outside of the pork.

3. Set the air fryer to 400°F. Place the tenderloin in the air fryer basket and cook for 8 minutes. Flip the meat and cook for 8 to 13 minutes more, until an instant-read thermometer reads 145°F in the thickest part.

4. Place the tenderloin on a plate and tent with a piece of aluminum foil. Allow the meat to rest for 5 to 10 minutes, then slice and serve warm.

Air Fryer tip: If you're working with a smaller air fryer model, use the largest tenderloin that will fit in your basket, and rely on the instant-read thermometer to adjust the cooking time accordingly.

PER SERVING: Total calories: 395; Total fat: 22g; Total carbohydrates: 1g; Fiber: 1g; Erythritol: 2g; Net carbs: <1g; Protein: 45g

MACROS: 50% Fat; 46% Protein; 4% Carbs

Sausage and Zucchini Lasagna

PREP TIME: **25 MINUTES** | COOK TIME: **56 MINUTES TO 1 HOUR** |
TEMPERATURE: **325°F**

Lasagna has always been one of my favorite meals. I love that I can make a keto-friendly version without sacrificing a smidgen of flavor. Hot sausage, earthy mushrooms, and creamy cheese in the confines of one dish is sheer bliss! **SERVES 4**

KID-FRIENDLY

1 zucchini

Avocado oil spray

6 ounces hot Italian sausage, casings removed

2 ounces mushrooms, stemmed and sliced

1 teaspoon minced garlic

1 cup keto-friendly marinara sauce

¾ cup ricotta cheese

1 cup shredded fontina cheese, divided

½ cup finely grated Parmesan cheese

Sea salt

Freshly ground black pepper

Fresh basil, for garnish

1. Cut the zucchini into long thin slices using a mandoline slicer or sharp knife. Spray both sides of the slices with oil.

2. Place the slices in a single layer in the air fryer basket, working in batches if necessary. Set the air fryer to 325°F and cook for 4 to 6 minutes, until most of the moisture has been released from the zucchini.

3. Place a large skillet over medium-high heat. Crumble the sausage into the hot skillet and cook for 6 minutes, breaking apart the meat with the back of a spoon. Remove the sausage from the skillet, leaving any fats that remain. Add the mushrooms to the skillet and cook for 10 minutes, until the liquid nearly evaporates. Add the garlic and cook for 1 minute more. Stir in the marinara and cook for 2 more minutes.

4. In a medium bowl, combine the ricotta cheese, ½ cup of fontina cheese, Parmesan cheese, and salt and pepper to taste.

5. Spread ¼ cup of the meat sauce in the bottom of a deep 7-inch pan (or other pan that fits inside your air fryer). Top with half of the zucchini slices. Add half of the cheese mixture. Top the cheese with half of the remaining meat sauce. Layer the remaining zucchini over the meat sauce and top with the remaining cheese mixture. Top the lasagna with the remaining ½ cup of fontina cheese.

6. Cover the lasagna with aluminum foil or parchment paper and place it in the air fryer. Cook for 25 minutes. Remove the foil and cook for 8 to 10 minutes more.

7. Allow the lasagna to rest for 15 minutes before cutting and serving. Garnish with basil.

PER SERVING: Total calories: 454; Total fat: 31g; Total carbohydrates: 11g; Fiber: 2g; Erythritol: 0g; Net carbs: 9g; Protein: 33g

MACROS: 61% Fat; 29% Protein; 10% Carbs

Smoky Pork Tenderloin

PREP TIME: **5 MINUTES** | COOK TIME: **19 TO 22 MINUTES** | TEMPERATURE: **400°F**

The air fryer shines here, delivering tender, juicy, perfectly browned pork tenderloin. When you need a fast meal, this never fails to satisfy. Serve this with Lemon-Garlic Mushrooms (page 39) or Parmesan-Rosemary Radishes (page 49).   SERVES 6

QUICK

KID-FRIENDLY

5-INGREDIENT

1½ pounds pork tenderloin

1 tablespoon avocado oil

1 teaspoon chili powder

1 teaspoon smoked paprika

1 teaspoon garlic powder

1 teaspoon sea salt

1 teaspoon freshly ground black pepper

1. Pierce the tenderloin all over with a fork and rub the oil all over the meat.

2. In a small dish, stir together the chili powder, smoked paprika, garlic powder, salt, and pepper.

3. Rub the spice mixture all over the tenderloin.

4. Set the air fryer to 400°F. Place the pork in the air fryer basket and cook for 10 minutes. Flip the tenderloin and cook for 9 to 12 minutes more, until an instant-read thermometer reads at least 145°F.

5. Allow the tenderloin to rest for 5 minutes, then slice and serve.

Air Fryer tip: If you're working with a smaller-capacity air fryer, use the largest tenderloin that will fit in your basket, and rely on the instant-read thermometer to adjust the cooking time accordingly.

PER SERVING: Total calories: 255; Total fat: 12g; Total carbohydrates: 1g; Fiber: <1g; Erythritol: 0g; Net carbs: 1g; Protein: 34g

MACROS: 42% Fat; 53% Protein; 5% Carbs

Pork Taco Bowls

PREP TIME: **15 MINUTES, PLUS 30 MINUTES TO MARINATE** | COOK TIME: **13 TO 16 MINUTES** | TEMPERATURE: **400°F**

I often like to double the meat in this recipe so we can repurpose it the next day. I've used it on everything from pizzas to low-carb wraps. If you would like to kick up the heat a bit, pickled jalapeños are great here. **SERVES 4**

KID-FRIENDLY

- **2 tablespoons avocado oil**
- **2 tablespoons freshly squeezed lime juice**
- **1 pound boneless pork shoulder**
- **2 tablespoons Taco Seasoning (page 167)**
- **½ small head cabbage, cored and thinly sliced**
- **Sea salt**
- **Freshly ground black pepper**
- **1 cup shredded Cheddar cheese**
- **¼ cup diced red onion**
- **¼ cup diced tomatoes**
- **1 avocado, sliced**
- **1 lime, cut into wedges**

1. In a small dish, whisk together the avocado oil and lime juice.

2. Pierce the pork all over with a fork and spread half of the oil mixture over it. Sprinkle with the taco seasoning and allow to sit at room temperature for 30 minutes.

3. Place the cabbage in a large bowl and toss with the remaining oil mixture. Season with salt and pepper.

4. Set the air fryer to 400°F. Place the pork in the air fryer basket and cook for 13 to 16 minutes, until an instant-read thermometer reads 145°F.

5. Allow the pork to rest for 10 minutes, then chop or shred the meat.

6. Place the cabbage in serving bowls. Top each serving with some pork, Cheddar cheese, red onion, tomatoes, and avocado. Serve with lime wedges.

PER SERVING: Total calories: 521; Total fat: 41g; Total carbohydrates: 17g; Fiber: 7g; Erythritol: 0g; Net carbs: 10g; Protein: 25g

MACROS: 71% Fat; 19% Protein; 10% Carbs

Tomato and Bacon Zoodles

PREP TIME: **10 MINUTES** | COOK TIME: **15 TO 22 MINUTES** | TEMPERATURE: **400°F**

This recipe came about as a happy accident in my kitchen. It was late on a Friday, and my kitchen and pantry were dreadfully bare. I threw together what I had on hand, and this simple dish was born. The smoky flavor of the bacon pairs so well with the salty and sweet cheeses. SERVES 2

FAVORITE

8 ounces sliced bacon

½ cup grape tomatoes

1 large zucchini, spiralized

½ cup ricotta cheese

¼ cup heavy (whipping) cream

⅓ cup finely grated Parmesan cheese, plus more for serving

Sea salt

Freshly ground black pepper

1. Set the air fryer to 400°F. Arrange the bacon strips in a single layer in the air fryer basket—some overlapping is okay because the bacon will shrink, but cook in batches if needed. Cook for 8 minutes. Flip the bacon strips and cook for 2 to 5 minutes more, until the bacon is crisp. Remove the bacon from the air fryer.

2. Put the tomatoes in the air fryer basket and cook for 3 to 5 minutes, until they are just starting to burst. Remove the tomatoes from the air fryer.

3. Put the zucchini noodles in the air fryer and cook for 2 to 4 minutes, to the desired doneness.

4. Meanwhile, combine the ricotta, heavy cream, and Parmesan in a saucepan over medium-low heat. Cook, stirring often, until warm and combined.

5. Crumble the bacon. Place the zucchini, bacon, and tomatoes in a bowl. Toss with the ricotta sauce. Season with salt and pepper, and sprinkle with additional Parmesan.

PER SERVING: Total calories: 535; Total fat: 40g; Total carbohydrates: 11g; Fiber: 2g; Erythritol: 0g; Net carbs: 9g; Protein: 35g

MACROS: 67% Fat; 26% Protein; 7% Carbs

Jalapeño Popper Pork Chops

PREP TIME: **15 MINUTES** | COOK TIME: **6 TO 8 MINUTES** | TEMPERATURE: **400°F**

Jalapeños, cream cheese, and pork may not be a classic combination, but sometimes it is fun to mix things up. This recipe will have you doing a happy dance. I'm all for experimentation in the kitchen. You never know what new culinary delight you may discover. **SERVES 4**

QUICK

1¾ pounds bone-in, center-cut loin pork chops

Sea salt

Freshly ground black pepper

6 ounces cream cheese, at room temperature

4 ounces sliced bacon, cooked and crumbled

4 ounces Cheddar cheese, shredded

1 jalapeño, seeded and diced

1 teaspoon garlic powder

1. Cut a pocket into each pork chop, lengthwise along the side, making sure not to cut it all the way through. Season the outside of the chops with salt and pepper.

2. In a small bowl, combine the cream cheese, bacon, Cheddar cheese, jalapeño, and garlic powder. Divide this mixture among the pork chops, stuffing it into the pocket of each chop.

3. Set the air fryer to 400°F. Place the pork chops in the air fryer basket in a single layer, working in batches if necessary. Cook for 3 minutes. Flip the chops and cook for 3 to 5 minutes more, until an instant-read thermometer reads 145°F.

4. Allow the chops to rest for 5 minutes, then serve warm.

PER SERVING: Total calories: 656; Total fat: 40g; Total carbohydrates: 4g; Fiber: <1g; Erythritol: 0g; Net carbs: 3g; Protein: 14g

MACROS: 55% Fat; 9% Protein; 36% Carbs

Bacon Five Ways

PREP TIME: **5 MINUTES** | COOK TIME: **10 TO 13 MINUTES** | TEMPERATURE: **400°F**

Is there anything better than perfectly crispy bacon? While plain bacon is absolutely delicious, sometimes it is fun to take things to the next level in terms of flavor. Here are five fun ways to elevate your bacon game. Pick from the following variations and use the same method for each.   SERVES 4

QUICK

KID-FRIENDLY

FAVORITE

5-INGREDIENT

Seasoning ingredients (see chart on page 149)

8 ounces sliced bacon

1. Combine the seasonings in a small bowl and brush or sprinkle the mixture over both sides of the bacon slices.

2. Set the air fryer to 400°F. Arrange the bacon in a single layer in the air fryer basket (some overlapping is okay because the bacon will shrink, but cook in batches if necessary).

3. Cook for 8 minutes. Flip the bacon strips and cook for 2 to 5 minutes more, until the bacon is crisp. Total cooking time will depend on the thickness of your bacon.

VARIATION	SEASONING INGREDIENTS
Maple	2 tablespoons maple syrup substitute, such as ChocZero sugar-free maple syrup ½ teaspoon freshly ground black pepper
Barbecue	2 tablespoons brown sugar substitute 1 teaspoon chili powder ½ teaspoon ground cumin ½ teaspoon smoked paprika
Sweet and Spicy	1 tablespoon brown sugar substitute ½ teaspoon freshly ground black pepper ⅛ teaspoon cayenne pepper
Maple-Sesame	2 tablespoons maple syrup substitute, such as ChocZero sugar-free maple syrup 1 teaspoon sesame oil 1 teaspoon sesame seeds
Balsamic	1 tablespoon balsamic vinegar ½ teaspoon garlic powder

Cooking tip: Bacon can vary wildly in terms of cooking time, depending on the brand and the thickness of the slices. Make sure you keep a close eye on it the first time you cook your favorite brand in the air fryer.

PER SERVING: Total calories: 124; Total fat: 8g; Total carbohydrates: 8g; Fiber: 7g; Erythritol: 0g; Net carbs: 1g; Protein: 9g

MACROS: 58% Fat; 29% Protein; 13% Carbs

Mini Peanut Butter
Tarts, page 156

8

Desserts & Staples

Chocolate Nut Pies

PREP TIME: **15 MINUTES** | COOK TIME: **25 MINUTES** | TEMPERATURE: **300°F**

Ready for something to swoon over? When I first made these little pies, I was instantly blown away by the deliciousness of them. They tip their hat to a pecan pie, but the additions of macadamia nuts and chocolate make them delightfully unique. Store them in the refrigerator for up to a week or in the freezer for up to 3 months.   SERVES 10

KID-FRIENDLY

VEGETARIAN

1¼ cups pecans

½ teaspoon sea salt

1 egg white

1¼ cups macadamia nuts, pecans, or a combination

⅓ cup plus 2 tablespoons stevia-sweetened chocolate chips, such as Lily's Sweets brand, divided

½ cup brown sugar substitute, such as Sukrin Gold

3 tablespoons maple syrup alternative, such as ChocZero sugar-free maple syrup

2 tablespoons unsalted butter

2 tablespoons heavy (whipping) cream

1 teaspoon vanilla extract

2 large eggs, beaten

1. Place the pecans and salt in the bowl of a food processor. Process until the nuts are very finely chopped. Transfer to a small bowl.

2. Place the egg white in the bowl of an electric mixer, and mix at high speed until stiff peaks form. Stir the egg white into the chopped pecans. Press the mixture into the bottom of 10 silicone muffin cups.

3. Place the muffin cups in the air fryer basket in a single layer, working in batches if necessary. Set the air fryer to 300°F and cook for 7 minutes. Remove the basket from the air fryer. Allow the muffin cups to cool slightly before removing them from the basket.

4. While the crusts are cooling, pulse the macadamia nuts in the food processor until coarsely chopped. Transfer to a

medium bowl and toss with 2 tablespoons of chocolate chips. Divide the mixture among the muffin cups.

5. Place the brown sugar substitute, maple syrup, and butter in a small saucepan over medium-high heat. Cook until the butter is melted and the sugars are dissolved. Stir in the cream and vanilla. Remove the pan from the heat and allow the mixture to cool slightly, then stir in the beaten eggs.

6. Pour the mixture over the nuts in the silicone cups, and return the cups to the air fryer basket. Set the air fryer to 300°F and cook for 12 minutes. Remove the basket from the air fryer. Once the pies are cool enough to handle, remove them from the basket.

7. Place the remaining ⅓ cup of chocolate chips in a glass bowl, and heat them in the microwave for about 1 minute, until melted. Stir well. (You can also melt the chocolate in the top of a double boiler.) Drizzle the chocolate over the pies and allow it to set before serving.

Substitution tip: Feel free to substitute any keto-friendly nuts, such as Brazil nuts, walnuts, or hazelnuts, in this recipe.

PER SERVING: Total calories: 332; Total fat: 30g; Total carbohydrates: 29g; Fiber: 9g; Erythritol: 10g; Net carbs: 10g; Protein: 4g
MACROS: 81% Fat; 5% Protein; 14% Carbs

Pecan Squares

PREP TIME: **20 MINUTES** | COOK TIME: **22 MINUTES** | TEMPERATURE: **325°F**

These chewy squares are rich and satisfying. When I serve them at parties, no one suspects that they are low-carb and sugar-free. If I could have just one dessert from now until the end of time, these squares would probably be it. SERVES 8

KID-FRIENDLY

VEGETARIAN

FAVORITE

1 cup finely ground blanched almond flour

1½ tablespoons Swerve Confectioners sweetener

5 tablespoons cold unsalted butter, cut into cubes

3 teaspoons pure vanilla extract, divided

¼ cup (4 tablespoons) unsalted butter, at room temperature

½ cup brown sugar substitute, such as Sukrin Gold

¼ cup maple syrup substitute, such as ChocZero sugar-free maple syrup

1 tablespoon heavy (whipping) cream

1¼ cups chopped pecans or other keto-friendly nuts (see page Substitution tip on page 153)

1. Line a 7-inch pan that is at least 2 inches deep with parchment paper. If you have it, a small springform pan works beautifully here. Otherwise, use enough parchment paper so that you have some overhang to help you lift the pastry from the pan once it has cooled.

2. Stir together the almond flour and Swerve in the bowl of a stand mixer. Add the cold butter and 1 teaspoon of vanilla, and beat until the mixture comes together, 3 to 4 minutes.

3. Press the crust into the prepared pan. Place the pan in the air fryer basket and set the air fryer to 325°F. Cook for 8 minutes. Remove the basket from the air fryer and allow the crust to cool.

4. While the crust cooks, combine the ¼ cup of butter, brown sugar substitute, and maple syrup substitute in a saucepan over medium heat. Cook until the butter is melted and the mixture is thick and bubbly, about 5 minutes. Stir in the heavy cream, remaining 2 teaspoons of vanilla, and chopped pecans.

5. Pour the mixture on top of the crust. Place the basket back in the air fryer and cook for 14 minutes or until set.

6. Remove the pan from the air fryer and let cool completely. Carefully remove the pastry from the pan and cut it into squares.

Cooking tip: However tempting, resist the urge to cut these while they are warm—they will fall apart if they are not completely cool.

PER SERVING: Total calories: 350; Total fat: 34g; Total carbohydrates: 28g; Fiber: 10g; Erythritol: 15g; Net carbs: 3g; Protein: 5g

MACROS: 87% Fat; 6% Protein; 7% Carbs

Mini Peanut Butter Tarts

PREP TIME: **25 MINUTES, PLUS 45 MINUTES TO FREEZE** | COOK TIME: **12 TO 15 MINUTES** | TEMPERATURE: **300°F**

The classic combination of chocolate and peanut butter never fails to disappoint. Both children and adults love these little tarts. They will leave everyone's taste buds singing—whether they're keto or not.   SERVES 8

KID-FRIENDLY

VEGETARIAN

1 cup pecans

1 cup finely ground blanched almond flour

2 tablespoons unsalted butter, at room temperature

½ cup plus 2 tablespoons Swerve Confectioners sweetener, divided

½ cup heavy (whipping) cream

2 tablespoons mascarpone cheese

4 ounces cream cheese

½ cup sugar-free peanut butter

1 teaspoon pure vanilla extract

⅛ teaspoon sea salt

½ cup stevia-sweetened chocolate chips, such as Lily's Sweets brand

1 tablespoon coconut oil

¼ cup chopped peanuts or pecans

1. Place the pecans in the bowl of a food processor; process until they are finely ground.

2. Transfer the ground pecans to a medium bowl and stir in the almond flour. Add the butter and 2 tablespoons of Swerve, and stir until the mixture becomes wet and crumbly.

3. Divide the mixture among 8 silicone muffin cups, pressing the crust firmly with your fingers into the bottom and part way up the sides of each cup.

4. Arrange the muffin cups in the air fryer basket, working in batches if necessary. Set the air fryer to 300°F and cook for 12 to 15 minutes, until the crusts begin to brown. Remove the cups from the air fryer and set them aside to cool.

5. In the bowl of a stand mixer, combine the heavy cream and mascarpone cheese. Beat until peaks form. Transfer to a large bowl.

6. In the same stand mixer bowl, combine the cream cheese, peanut butter, remaining ½ cup of Swerve, vanilla, and salt. Beat at medium-high speed until smooth.

7. Reduce the speed to low and add the heavy cream mixture back a spoonful at a time, beating after each addition.

8. Spoon the peanut butter mixture over the crusts, and freeze the tarts for 30 minutes.

9. Place the chocolate chips and coconut oil in the top of a double boiler over high heat. Stir until melted, then remove from the heat.

10. Drizzle the melted chocolate over the peanut butter tarts. Top with the chopped nuts and freeze the tarts for another 15 minutes, until set.

11. Store the peanut butter tarts in an airtight container in the refrigerator for up to 1 week or in the freezer for up to 1 month.

Cooking tip: I like to use silicone muffin cups here because it is very easy to remove the tarts from them. If you prefer, you can use a well-greased air fryer muffin tin instead.

PER SERVING: Total calories: 491; Total fat: 46g; Total carbohydrates: 30g; Fiber: 7g; Erythritol: 15g; Net carbs: 8g; Protein: 11g

MACROS: 84% Fat; 9% Protein; 7% Carbs

Chocolate Chip–Pecan Biscotti

PREP TIME: **15 MINUTES** | COOK TIME: **20 TO 22 MINUTES** | TEMPERATURE: **325°F, THEN 300°F**

With three children, quiet moments are a rare treat. When I can sneak away, I love to linger over a cup of coffee with a good book. Nothing makes these moments more luxurious than a sweet nibble such as a homemade biscotti. It elevates any occasion to something special.   SERVES 10

KID FRIENDLY

VEGETARIAN

- 1¼ cups finely ground blanched almond flour
- ¾ teaspoon baking powder
- ½ teaspoon xanthan gum
- ¼ teaspoon sea salt
- 3 tablespoons unsalted butter, at room temperature
- ⅓ cup Swerve Confectioners sweetener
- 1 large egg, beaten
- 1 teaspoon pure vanilla extract
- ⅓ cup chopped pecans
- ¼ cup stevia-sweetened chocolate chips, such as Lily's Sweets brand
- Melted stevia-sweetened chocolate chips and chopped pecans, for topping (optional)

1. In a large bowl, combine the almond flour, baking powder, xanthan gum, and salt.

2. Line a 7-inch cake pan that fits inside your air fryer with parchment paper.

3. In the bowl of a stand mixer, beat together the butter and Swerve. Add the beaten egg and vanilla, and beat for about 3 minutes.

4. Add the almond flour mixture to the butter-and-egg mixture; beat until just combined.

5. Stir in the pecans and chocolate chips.

6. Transfer the dough to the prepared pan, and press it into the bottom.

7. Set the air fryer to 325°F and cook for 12 minutes. Remove from the air fryer and let cool for 15 minutes. Using a sharp knife, cut the cookie into thin strips, then return the strips to the cake pan with the bottom sides facing up.

8. Set the air fryer to 300°F. Cook for 8 to 10 minutes.

9. Remove from the air fryer and let cool completely on a wire rack. If desired, dip one side of each biscotti piece into melted chocolate chips, and top with chopped pecans.

PER SERVING: Total calories: 148; Total fat: 14g; Total carbohydrates: 11g; Fiber: 2g; Erythritol: 6g; Net carbs: 3g; Protein: 4g

MACROS: 85% Fat; 11% Protein; 4% Carbs

Almond Flour Cinnamon Rolls

PREP TIME: **20 MINUTES, PLUS 30 MINUTES TO CHILL** | COOK TIME: **16 TO 18 MINUTES** | TEMPERATURE: **300°F**

Cinnamon rolls are pure comfort food, and this recipe is perfect for a cool fall afternoon treat. It has all the taste of the classic rolls you love, with ingredients that will leave you feeling great. Don't skip the almond glaze—it transforms this recipe from breakfast to dessert in my book.   SERVES 8

KID-FRIENDLY

VEGETARIAN

FAVORITE

3 tablespoons unsalted butter, at room temperature

½ cup brown sugar substitute, such as Sukrin Gold

1 teaspoon ground cinnamon

1½ cups finely ground blanched almond flour

¼ teaspoon sea salt

¼ teaspoon baking soda

¼ teaspoon xanthan gum

1 large egg, at room temperature

2 tablespoons unsalted butter, melted and cooled

1 tablespoon Swerve Confectioners sweetener

Avocado oil spray

Almond Glaze (page 162), for serving

1. In the bowl of a stand mixer, beat together the room temperature butter, brown sugar substitute, and cinnamon. Set aside.

2. In a large bowl, combine the almond flour, salt, baking soda, and xanthan gum.

3. In a separate bowl, beat the egg. Stir in the cooled melted butter and Swerve until combined.

4. Add the egg-and-butter mixture to the flour mixture and knead with clean hands until the dough is smooth.

5. Spray a large bowl with oil, add the dough, and turn it to coat in the oil. Cover and refrigerate for 30 minutes.

6. Place the dough on a piece of parchment paper and form it into a rectangle. Put another piece of parchment on top of the dough and roll out the dough to a large rectangle, about ¼-inch thick.

7. Spread the butter and brown sugar mixture on top of the dough, and then roll up the dough from the long side. (Use the parchment paper to help if needed.)

8. Slice the rolled dough into 8 equal-size pieces, and arrange these in a parchment paper–lined 7-inch cake pan that fits inside your air fryer.

9. Set the air fryer to 300°F. Cook for 16 to 18 minutes, until the tops of the rolls are lightly browned.

10. Let the rolls cool for 5 minutes, then invert them onto a plate. Sprinkle any cinnamon sugar mixture that has collected on the bottom of the pan over the top of the rolls.

11. Drizzle the Almond Glaze over the cinnamon rolls; serve warm.

Cooking tip: Feel free to make the recipe the night before. Spray the tops of the rolls with oil and cover them tightly with plastic wrap. Store leftovers in the refrigerator or freezer and reheat them before serving.

PER SERVING: Total calories: 193; Total fat: 18g; Total carbohydrates: 18g; Fiber: 2g; Erythritol: 14g; Net carbs: 2g; Protein: 5g

MACROS: 84% Fat; 10% Protein; 6% Carbs

Almond Glaze

PREP TIME: **5 MINUTES**

I love using this simple glaze to add an extra touch of sweetness to cinnamon rolls, Blueberry Muffins (page 25), and cookies. I use almond extract for an extra depth of flavor, but feel free to sub in additional vanilla extract instead. **SERVES 8**

QUICK

KID-FRIENDLY

VEGETARIAN

FAVORITE

5-INGREDIENT

½ cup Swerve Confectioners sweetener

½ tablespoon unsalted butter, at room temperature

2 to 3 tablespoons heavy (whipping) cream

¼ teaspoon almond extract

¼ teaspoon pure vanilla extract

1. Combine the Swerve, butter, 2 tablespoons of heavy cream, almond extract, and vanilla extract in a large bowl. Whisk until creamy, adding additional heavy cream as needed to achieve your preferred consistency.

2. Drizzle over cinnamon rolls, blueberry muffins, or cookies.

Substitution tip: Feel free to use other sweeteners that you prefer. If you use a granular sweetener, I recommend processing it for about 2 minutes in your food processor. This will help you avoid a gritty texture in the finished glaze.

PER SERVING: Total calories: 20; Total fat: 2g; Total carbohydrates: 12g; Fiber: 0g; Erythritol: 12g; Net carbs: 0g; Protein: <1g

MACROS: 90% Fat; <1% Protein; 9% Carbs

Elevated Tartar Sauce

PREP TIME: **5 MINUTES**

I am all about the sauces, and it doesn't get much better than this tartar sauce. It is crunchy, sweet, creamy, and tangy all at once. This recipe is fantastic paired with shrimp and fish. While it has a few more ingredients than many other tartar sauce recipes, it comes together in a flash, and the payoff is more than worth an extra 3 minutes.   SERVES 8

QUICK

KID-FRIENDLY

VEGETARIAN

½ cup sugar-free mayonnaise (homemade, page 164, or store-bought)

¼ cup diced dill pickles

1 shallot, diced

2 tablespoons drained capers, rinsed and chopped

2 teaspoons Swerve Confectioners or other keto-approved sweetener

2 teaspoons dill pickle juice

1 teaspoon dried dill

½ teaspoon sea salt

½ teaspoon freshly ground black pepper

⅛ teaspoon cayenne pepper

1. In a medium bowl, mix together the mayonnaise, pickles, shallot, capers, Swerve, pickle juice, dill, salt, pepper, and cayenne pepper until thoroughly combined.

2. Cover and refrigerate until ready to serve.

Cooking tip: Store this tartar sauce in an airtight container in the refrigerator for up to 1 week.

PER SERVING: Total calories: 93; Total fat: 11g; Total carbohydrates: 2g; Fiber: <1g; Erythritol: 1g; Net carbs: 1g; Protein: <1g

MACROS: 100% Fat; <1% Protein; <1% Carbs

Mayonnaise Three Ways

PREP TIME: **10 MINUTES**

Mayonnaise is a staple on a keto diet, but most store-bought versions have added sugars. Those that don't include sugar are either ridiculously expensive or full of canola and soybean oils, which are not keto-friendly. Making mayonnaise at home is a tasty and economical solution. This first recipe is for a basic mayo; you can dress it up with the three variations that follow. For all the variations, place the additional ingredients in a food processor with 1 recipe of basic mayonnaise and process until smooth. **SERVES 16**

QUICK

KID-FRIENDLY

VEGETARIAN

FAVORITE

5-INGREDIENT

1 large egg, at room temperature

1½ tablespoons freshly squeezed lemon juice

½ teaspoon mustard powder

1 cup avocado oil

½ teaspoon sea salt

¼ teaspoon freshly ground white pepper

Additional ingredients (see chart, optional)

1. Place the egg, lemon juice, and mustard powder in a blender or food processor; process until combined.

2. With the motor running, in a thin stream, SLOWLY add the avocado oil. It is important to be patient here. It should take you about 3 minutes to fully incorporate the oil.

3. Once the mayonnaise has come together, add the salt and pepper and process until combined.

4. Add the additional variation ingredients (if using) and process until well combined.

VARIATION	ADDITIONAL INGREDIENTS
Caper Mayonnaise	2 tablespoons capers, drained 2 teaspoons Dijon mustard 2 teaspoons freshly squeezed lemon juice ¼ teaspoon freshly ground black pepper
Horseradish Mayonnaise	⅓ cup prepared horseradish, more or less to taste ¼ teaspoon cayenne pepper
Sriracha Mayonnaise	2 tablespoons Sriracha sauce, more or less to taste 1 teaspoon minced garlic ¼ teaspoon freshly ground black pepper

Cooking tip: Make sure you bring all your ingredients to room temperature before making mayonnaise. If you would like to use an immersion blender to make this recipe, I recommend using a wide mouth mason jar or a tall flat-bottomed glass. The mayonnaise will keep for up to 10 days in an airtight container in the refrigerator.

PER SERVING (BASIC): Total calories: 124; Total fat: 14g; Total carbohydrates: <1g; Fiber: 0g; Erythritol: 0g; Net carbs: 0g; Protein: <1g

MACROS: 100% Fat; <1% Protein; <1% Carbs

Creamy Sausage Gravy

PREP TIME: **10 MINUTES** | COOK TIME: **13 MINUTES**

Without question, my favorite weekend breakfast is this creamy keto gravy served with my Down Home Biscuits (page 22). It is the kind of comfort food that never gets old, and it's a company-worthy dish that everyone—even those not on a low-carb diet—will crave again and again.   SERVES 8

QUICK

KID-FRIENDLY

FAVORITE

1 tablespoon unsalted butter

12 ounces breakfast sausage, casings removed

⅓ cup chopped onion

1 cup chicken broth

1 cup heavy (whipping) cream

8 ounces cream cheese, cut into cubes

¼ teaspoon xanthan gum

1½ teaspoons garlic powder

½ teaspoon sea salt

½ teaspoon freshly ground black pepper

1. Melt the butter in a large saucepan over medium-high heat. Add the sausage and cook, using a spoon to break up the meat, for about 6 minutes or until the sausage is no longer pink. Add the onion and cook for 2 minutes. Stir in the broth, heavy cream, cream cheese, and xanthan gum.

2. Bring the mixture to a simmer, whisking constantly. Reduce the heat to medium-low and cook until the mixture thickens, about 5 minutes.

3. Stir in the garlic powder, salt, and pepper; serve hot.

PER SERVING: Total calories: 331; Total fat: 32g; Total carbohydrates: 5g; Fiber: <1g; Erythritol: 0g; Net carbs: 5g; Protein: 8g

MACROS: 87% Fat; 10% Protein; 3% Carbs

Taco Seasoning

PREP TIME: **5 MINUTES**

Sure, you can buy taco seasoning, but why would you, when making your own is so easy (and less expensive)? Plus, most commercially available spice blends have anti-caking agents that can contain hidden carbs.   **SERVES 8**

QUICK

KID-FRIENDLY

VEGETARIAN

3 tablespoons chili powder

1½ tablespoons ground cumin

1½ tablespoons garlic powder

1 tablespoon sea salt

2 teaspoons onion powder

2 teaspoons smoked paprika

2 teaspoons dried oregano

1 teaspoon freshly ground black pepper

¼ teaspoon cayenne pepper

1. In a small bowl, combine the chili powder, cumin, garlic powder, salt, onion powder, smoked paprika, oregano, black pepper, and cayenne pepper.

2. Transfer to a small, airtight jar, seal, and store in your pantry.

Variation tip: I am a big fan of smoked paprika, but if you don't have it on hand, feel free to substitute with sweet paprika. I like the moderate touch of heat from the cayenne pepper, but if you (or your children) are extremely sensitive to heat, just leave it out.

PER SERVING: Total calories: 23; Total fat: 1g; Total carbohydrates: 4g; Fiber: 2g; Erythritol: 0g; Net carbs: 2g; Protein: 1g

MACROS: 39% Fat; 17% Protein; 44% Carbs

Garlic Ranch Dressing

PREP TIME: **10 MINUTES**

This dressing will become a staple in your house, just like it is in mine! It keeps perfectly in the refrigerator for lunch all week and is so tasty you will find yourself getting excited for salad again. It also makes a great dip and is delicious with many of the Buffalo-sauced recipes in this book.   SERVES 12

QUICK

KID-FRIENDLY

VEGETARIAN

¼ cup heavy (whipping) cream

1 teaspoon apple cider vinegar

½ cup sugar-free mayonnaise (homemade, page 164, or store-bought)

½ cup sour cream

1 tablespoon minced garlic

1 teaspoon dried oregano

1 teaspoon onion powder

1 teaspoon sea salt

½ teaspoon dried dill

½ teaspoon freshly ground black pepper

Additional heavy cream or bone broth, for thinning

1. Whisk together the heavy cream and apple cider vinegar in a medium bowl until combined. Let the mixture rest for 10 minutes, then whisk in the mayonnaise, sour cream, garlic, oregano, onion powder, salt, dill, and pepper.

2. Thin the dressing to your desired consistency, using more heavy cream or bone broth (it will no longer be vegetarian if you use bone broth).

3. Transfer to an airtight container, and refrigerate for up to 1 week.

PER SERVING: Total calories: 103; Total fat: 11g; Total carbohydrates: 2g; Fiber: <1g; Erythritol: 0g; Net carbs: 2g; Protein: 1g

MACROS: 96% Fat; 3% Protein; 1% Carbs

Blue Cheese Dressing

PREP TIME: **5 MINUTES**

With almost no prep time, you've got a delicious dip or salad dressing that you will find yourself reaching for all week long. (That is, if it doesn't get eaten sooner.) This recipe isn't particularly fussy, so feel free to adjust it to your taste. Sometimes I increase the garlic and kick up the heat level with a touch of cayenne pepper. **SERVES 12**

QUICK

VEGETARIAN

¾ cup sugar-free mayonnaise (homemade, page 164, or store-bought)

¼ cup sour cream

½ cup heavy (whipping) cream

1 teaspoon minced garlic

1 tablespoon freshly squeezed lemon juice

1 tablespoon apple cider vinegar

1 teaspoon hot sauce

½ teaspoon sea salt

4 ounces blue cheese, crumbled (about ¾ cup)

1. In a medium bowl, whisk together the mayonnaise, sour cream, and heavy cream.

2. Stir in the garlic, lemon juice, apple cider vinegar, hot sauce, and sea salt.

3. Add the blue cheese crumbles, and stir until well combined.

4. Transfer to an airtight container, and refrigerate for up to 1 week.

Ingredient tip: Any blue cheese will work in this recipe, but I highly recommend going with the best quality that fits your budget. I like to buy a block and crumble it myself, as I find that the cheese has so much more flavor that way.

PER SERVING: Total calories: 171; Total fat: 18g; Total carbohydrates: 1g; Fiber: 0g; Erythritol: 0g; Net carbs: 1g; Protein: 2g

MACROS: 95% Fat; 5% Protein; 0% Carbs

Tzatziki Sauce

PREP TIME: **15 MINUTES**

Tzatziki sauce is a Greek dip traditionally made with yogurt; it is often found on gyros. Here, I've switched out the yogurt for sour cream to make the sauce more keto-friendly. Try it with meat or vegetables, or, if you like, thin it out with a touch of heavy cream and use it as a salad dressing.   SERVES 6

QUICK

KID-FRIENDLY

VEGETARIAN

FAVORITE

5-INGREDIENT

½ cucumber, seeded and finely chopped

½ teaspoon sea salt, plus additional for seasoning

¾ cup sour cream

1 tablespoon freshly squeezed lemon juice

1 tablespoon chopped fresh dill

3 garlic cloves, minced

1. Place the cucumber in a colander set in the sink or over a bowl, and sprinkle it with salt. Let stand for 10 minutes, then transfer the cucumber to a clean dishcloth and wring it out, extracting as much liquid as you can.

2. In a medium bowl, stir together the cucumber, sour cream, lemon juice, dill, garlic, and ½ teaspoon of salt.

3. Store the sauce in an airtight container in the refrigerator for up to 4 days.

PER SERVING: Total calories: 77; Total fat: 6g; Total carbohydrates: 3g; Fiber: <1g; Erythritol: 0g; Net carbs: 3g; Protein: 1g

MACROS: 70% Fat; 5% Protein; 25% Carbs

Fathead Pizza Dough

PREP TIME: **10 MINUTES**

Pizza is my ultimate quick dinner. This dough is simple to make and allows me to have pizza on the table in less than 30 minutes. You won't believe how tasty this pizza crust is—and the whole family will love it, too.   SERVES 8

QUICK

KID-FRIENDLY

VEGETARIAN

FAVORITE

5-INGREDIENT

6 ounces low-moisture mozzarella cheese, shredded (about 1½ cups)

2 ounces cream cheese, diced

1 large egg

1 cup finely ground blanched almond flour

½ teaspoon sea salt

¼ teaspoon freshly ground black pepper

1. Combine the mozzarella cheese and cream cheese in a medium saucepan over medium heat. Cook, stirring often, until the cheeses are melted.

2. Remove the pan from the heat and stir in the egg, almond flour, salt, and pepper.

3. Transfer the mixture to a sheet of parchment paper and knead the dough until it is well combined.

4. Place the dough between 2 sheets of parchment paper. Roll out the dough to your preferred thickness (or whatever thickness your recipe requires). Cook as directed to make pizza, calzones, or empanadas.

PER SERVING: Total calories: 173; Total fat: 15g; Total carbohydrates: 4g; Fiber: 2g; Erythritol: 0g; Net carbs: 2g; Protein: 10g

MACROS: 78% Fat; 22% Protein; 0% Carbs

AIR FRYER CHARTS

FRESH VEGETABLES	QUANTITY	TIME	TEMPERATURE	NOTES
Asparagus	1 pound	5 to 8 minutes	400°F	Trim off the ends before cooking
Broccoli florets	2 to 4 cups	5 to 8 minutes	400°F	Season with salt and pepper, and spray with oil
Brussels sprouts	2 cups	13 to 15 minutes	380°F	Halve the Brussels sprouts lengthwise first; coat with oil and seasonings
Cauliflower florets	2 to 4 cups	9 to 10 minutes	360°F	Coat with oil and seasonings
Eggplant	1 to 3 pounds	13 to 15 minutes	400°F	Chop or slice before cooking; spray with oil, and flip halfway through cooking time
Green beans	1 to 3 pounds	5 minutes	400°F	Spray with oil and shake halfway through cooking
Kale	1 bunch	10 to 12 minutes	275°F	Remove tough ribs. Coat the leaves with oil, and sprinkle with seasonings. Shake halfway through cooking.

Mushrooms	1 to 2 cups	5 to 8 minutes	400°F	Cut off stems before cooking
Onions	1 to 3 pounds	5 to 8 minutes	370°F	Chop before cooking
Peppers (bell)	1 to 2 cups	6 to 8 minutes	370°F	Cut into strips before cooking
Summer squash	1 pound	12 to 13 minutes	400°F	Chop first, then brush with cooking oil and seasonings
Zucchini	1 to 3 pounds	10 to 12 minutes	370°F	Chop first, then brush with cooking oil and seasonings

CHICKEN	QUANTITY	TIME	TEMPERA-TURE	NOTES
Chicken breasts	Up to 4 (6-ounce) skinless breasts	12 to 14 minutes	400°F	Spray with oil, and flip halfway through cooking
Chicken drumettes	Up to 8 drumettes	20 minutes	400°F	Spray with oil, and shake halfway through cooking

(continued)

Chicken drumsticks	1 to 6 drumsticks	16 to 20 minutes	390°F	Spray with oil, and shake halfway through cooking
Chicken tenders	Up to 8 chicken tenders	8 to 10 minutes	375°F	Spray with oil, and shake halfway through cooking
Chicken thighs (bone-in)	Up to 4 (6-ounce) chicken thighs	22 minutes	380°F	Spray with oil, and shake halfway through cooking
Chicken thighs (boneless)	Up to 4 (6-ounce) chicken thighs	18 to 20 minutes	380°F	Spray with oil, and shake halfway through cooking
Whole chicken	1 (2-pound) whole chicken	75 minutes	360°F	Coat with oil and seasonings before cooking
Whole chicken wings	Up to 8 wings	15 to 20 minutes	400°F	Spray with oil, and shake halfway through cooking

BEEF	QUANTITY	TIME	TEMPERA-TURE	NOTES
Burgers	¼ to 1 pound	8 to 10 minutes	400°F	Do not stack; flip halfway through cooking
Filet mignon	Up to 4 (6-ounce) steaks	8 to 10 minutes	360°F	Time will vary depending on desired doneness; use an instant-read thermometer and cook to 125°F for rare, 135°F for medium-rare, 145°F for medium, 155°F for medium-well, and 160° F for well-done
Flank steak	2 pounds	8 to 10 minutes	400°F	Time will vary depending on desired doneness; use an instant-read thermometer and cook to 125°F for rare, 135°F for medium-rare, 145°F for medium, 155°F for medium-well, and 160°F for well-done

(continued)

Meatballs	Up to 25	7 to 10 minutes	380°F	Do not stack; flip halfway through cooking
Rib eye steak	Up to 4 (6-ounce) steaks	10 to 15 minutes	380°F	Time will vary depending on desired doneness; use an instant-read thermometer and cook to 125°F for rare, 135°F for medium-rare, 145°F for medium, 155°F for medium-well, and 160°F for well-done
Sirloin steak	Up to 4 (6-ounce) steaks	12 to 14 minutes	400°F	Time will vary depending on desired doneness; use an instant-read thermometer and cook to 125°F for rare, 135°F for medium-rare, 145°F for medium, 155°F for medium-well, and 160°F for well-done

PORK AND LAMB	QUANTITY	TIME	TEMPERATURE	NOTES
Bacon	6 strips	7 to 10 minutes	400°F	Do not stack; flip halfway through cooking
Lamb chops	¼ to 1 pound	10 to 12 minutes	400°F	Do not stack; flip halfway through cooking
Pork chops	¼ to 1 pound	12 to 15 minutes	380°F	Spray with oil, and flip halfway through cooking
Pork loin	¼ to 1 pound	50 to 60 minutes	360°F	Sprinkle with seasonings, and flip halfway through cooking
Pork tenderloin	¼ to 1 pound	12 to 15 minutes	390°F	Drizzle with olive oil, and cook whole
Rack of lamb	¼ to 1 pound	22 to 25 minutes	380°F	Do not stack; flip halfway through cooking
Sausages (links)	¼ to 1 pound	13 to 15 minutes	380°F	Prick holes in sausages before cooking
Sausages (patties)	Up to 6 patties	13 to 15 minutes	380°F	Do not stack; flip halfway through cooking

(continued)

AIR FRYER CHARTS *(continued)*

FISH AND SEAFOOD	QUANTITY	TIME	TEMPERATURE	NOTES
Crab cakes	4 crab cakes	8 to 10 minutes	375°F	Toss with finely ground blanched almond flour, and coat with oil
Fish fillet	¼ to 1 pound	10 to 12 minutes	320°F	Brush with oil, and sprinkle with seasonings
Salmon	¼ to 1 pound	10 to 12 minutes	320°F	Brush with oil, and sprinkle with seasonings
Scallops	¼ to 1 pound	5 to 7 minutes	320°F	Brush with oil, and sprinkle with seasonings
Shrimp	¼ to 1 pound	7 to 8 minutes	400°F	Peel and devein; brush with oil and sprinkle with seasonings

MEASUREMENT CONVERSIONS

Volume Equivalents (Liquid)

US STANDARD	US STANDARD (OUNCES)	METRIC (APPROXIMATE)
2 tablespoons	1 fl. oz.	30 mL
¼ cup	2 fl. oz.	60 mL
½ cup	4 fl. oz.	120 mL
1 cup	8 fl. oz.	240 mL
1½ cups	12 fl. oz.	355 mL
2 cups or 1 pint	16 fl. oz.	475 mL
4 cups or 1 quart	32 fl. oz.	1 L
1 gallon	128 fl. oz.	4 L

Oven Temperatures

FAHRENHEIT (F)	CELSIUS (C) (APPROXIMATE)
250°F	120°C
300°F	150°C
325°F	165°C
350°F	180°C
375°F	190°C
400°F	200°C
425°F	220°C
450°F	230°C

Volume Equivalents (Dry)

US STANDARD	METRIC (APPROXIMATE)
⅛ teaspoon	0.5 mL
¼ teaspoon	1 mL
½ teaspoon	2 mL
¾ teaspoon	4 mL
1 teaspoon	5 mL
1 tablespoon	15 mL
¼ cup	59 mL
⅓ cup	79 mL
½ cup	118 mL
⅔ cup	156 mL
¾ cup	177 mL
1 cup	235 mL
2 cups or 1 pint	475 mL
3 cups	700 mL
4 cups or 1 quart	1 L

Weight Equivalents

US STANDARD	METRIC (APPROXIMATE)
½ ounce	15 g
1 ounce	30 g
2 ounces	60 g
4 ounces	115 g
8 ounces	225 g
12 ounces	340 g
16 ounces or 1 pound	455 g

RESOURCES

If you are new to the keto lifestyle, you might want to dive deeper and learn more about it. Here are some great books and websites that will help you do that.

BOOKS

The Obesity Code: Unlocking the Secrets of Weight Loss, by Dr. Jason Fung (Greystone Books, 2016)

Keto Clarity: Your Definitive Guide to the Benefits of a Low-Carb, High-Fat Diet, by Jimmy Moore and Eric C. Westman, MD (Belt Publishing, 2014)

The Art and Science of Low Carbohydrate Living, by Stephen D. Phinney and Jeff S. Volek (Beyond Obesity, LLC, 2011)

The Keto Diet: The Complete Guide to a High-Fat Diet, by Leanne Vogel (Victory Belt Publishing, 2017)

WEBSITES

Visit me at kicking-carbs.com, and check out these other websites, which will help you on your keto journey:

AllDayIDreamAboutFood.com

HealthfulPursuit.com

IBreatheImHungry.com

LowCarbYum.com

PeaceLoveandLowCarb.com

WholesomeYum.com

INDEX

ACKNOWLEDGMENTS

A **LEX AND CHRISTIAN, YOU ARE** the best recipe tasters I could ask for. Your enthusiasm about this book was everything when I was exhausted and didn't feel like I could test another recipe. Thank you for all the kitchen cleanup, hugs, and encouragement. I am so proud of you both.

Skye, my sweet girl. You are my sunshine! Seeing you in your apron and chef's hat never fails to make my day. I cannot wait to continue our kitchen adventures and watch you grow. I could have never imagined all the ways in which you would complete our family.

Vincent, thank you for being there and supporting me throughout this journey. (And for not complaining about all the meat you had to eat that was cooked past rare.)

Mom and Dad, thank you for believing in me and always being there when I need you.

Thanks to Bridget Fitzgerald of Callisto Media for your support, patience, and editorial guidance.

Last but not least, I would like to thank my readers for allowing me to do what I love for the last eight years. I am forever grateful for your support.

ABOUT THE AUTHOR

WENDY POLISI is the passionate cook, photographer, and blogger behind WendyPolisi.com and Kicking-Carbs.com. When she is not in the kitchen, chances are you will find her at a theme park with her kids. She lives in Orlando, Florida, with her husband and three children.

CPSIA information can be obtained
at www.ICGtesting.com
Printed in the USA
BVHW021047160420
577668BV00013B/497